OVERCOMING
THE STRONGMAN

A HANDBOOK ON SPIRITUAL WARFARE

DR. RAVINDRA SHIWNANDAN

RAVINDRA SHIWNANDAN
Visit my website at www.herstellingaoggoc.org

Printed in the United States of America

First Printing: March 2019

Herstelling Assembly of God
Global Outreach Center
350-351 Herstelling, EBD, Guyana, South America

ISBN: 9781091638556

Dedicated to
all spiritual warriors who were mobilized and
trained to engage the enemy with powerful weapons, and are
tearing down the enemy's strongholds all over the earth.

"Enemy-occupied territory-----that is what this world is. Christianity is the story of how the rightful king has landed; you might say landed in disguise, and is calling us all to take part in a great campaign in sabotage."

—*C.S. Lewis*

CONTENTS

FOREWORD

Know Your Enemy. We are not to be ignorant of Satan's devices lest he take advantage of us.

In this book, *Overcoming The Strongman*, Dr. Shiwnandan has covered almost every area which had been previously hidden, though in plain sight. He has also shed light on some areas that have been overlooked by the church to her disadvantage.

He lays the foundation which exposes that this conflict is not localized to denominations or geography, but it is a universal human spiritual conflict.

Many topics covered in this work highlight events not generally referenced, for example *The Lausanne Covenant- Statement of Spiritual Warfare (1993).*

Dr. Shiwnandan's discipline as a medical doctor informs his exposition of the book's theme, particularly in the chapter on *Warfare Realities #3- Vision Affects Outcome*. Unlike many works written on the same theme; the writer gives consideration to the physiological and psychological dimensions as also being important in determining one's perspective which is key in overcoming the Strongman. The natural and psychological perceptions are aspects, in my estimation, that are rarely ever addressed in works on spiritual warfare.

Wherever or at whatever level you are in the conflict, *Overcoming The Strongman* will significantly benefit you, since it touches every aspect of spiritual warfare.

I consider Dr. Shiwnandan's book and knowledge on this aspect of spiritual warfare unparalleled. I strongly recommend this book as a resource not only for pastors or church leaders or workers but also for the serious students of the Bible and for the individual Christian who is seeking to live victoriously.

Bishop Louis I. Crawford
Senior Pastor
House of Prayer-Tucville Assembly of God

ACKNOWLEDGMENTS

First and foremost, I would like to thank God who has given me the power to believe in my passion and to pursue my dreams. He has blessed me with several gifts among which is the gift of writing. I thank Him for the insights and determination to complete this book.

I wish to thank everyone who helped me complete this book. Without their continued efforts and support, I would not have been able to bring this work to successful completion.

I thank my wife Michelle who endured hundreds of hours of my absence while I hibernated to write and adjust several drafts of my manuscript before deciding on this final one.

I want to express my gratitude to the many authors and ministries listed in the Reference page for the opportunity I had to review their material while writing this book. I humbly applaud their works and thank many of them for willingly allowing me to use their materials.

I appreciate the efforts of Chief and my sister Joyce who edited my manuscript. Their invaluable contributions will be cherished forever.

I thank Bishop Louis Crawford, the Executive Presbyter of the Assemblies of God in Guyana, for his prayerful support in this project. The applaud he gave on a review of my manuscript, the invitations to share the content of my book with his congregation, and the impressive Foreword he wrote mean the world to me.

For all those who spoke encouraging words along the way, thank you.

Ravindra Shiwnandan
2019

1. There's A Real War Raging!

Spiritual warfare, from a Christian's perspective, is the universal war between good and evil. It is the battle that started when Satan rebelled against God many millennia ago. The rebellion has continued ever since and is on, on a daily basis. This war has escalated to involve the Church and the world's systems, which is ruled by our spiritual enemy. Although this conflict exists on a global scale, it is also experienced individually by every Christian; conflict between the Holy Spirit and the lust of the flesh.

Spiritual warfare is not new; Christians have practiced spiritual warfare in varying ways throughout the history of Christianity, and through spiritual warfare, they actively take their stand against the preternatural evil forces which can intervene in human affairs.[1]

Over the years the desire to know more about spiritual warfare and the development of specific spiritual warfare techniques has generated much discussion in the church. Christians want to know more about what is in Jesus' statement when He said: *"the kingdom of heaven suffereth violence and the violent take it by force."(Matthew 11:12)*

In the year 1993, an international collaborative attempt was made by evangelicals and charismatics in the Lausanne Committee for World Evangelism, to reach some common agreements about spiritual warfare. The results of this consultation were presented as a Statement on Spiritual Warfare (1993)[2] which I will refer to at a

---

1 Arnold, Clinton E. (1997). 3 crucial questions about spiritual warfare. Grand Rapids, Mich.: Baker Publishing Group. p. 17. ISBN 0801057841.
2 Statement on Spiritual Warfare,
(1993)https://www.lausanne.org/content/statement/statement-on-

later time.

In the American revival tradition among evangelicals, prominent preachers such as D. L. Moody, Billy Sunday, R. A. Torrey and Billy Graham, have all affirmed their belief in the existence of the demonic and have recounted some of their own spiritual warfare encounters on occasions. John Livingstone Nevius; the Chinese missionary, was one of the most significant evangelical authorities on demonic possession in the nineteenth century. [3]

Also, during the late twentieth century, Drs. Mark I. Bubeck and Merrill Frederick Unger, two seasoned pastors and theologians, openly presented their response to widespread demonic phenomena and the subjects of demon possession. As a result, spiritual warfare became the topics of a *Christian Medical Association* symposium that was held in 1975.[4]

However, spiritual warfare is not limited to the Christian and the church; it has also been practiced by non-Christian and non-Christian countries.

According to the *Christian Broadcasting Network* commentator Carl Moeller, spiritual warfare is practiced even in North Korea; a country described as the most dangerous place on earth to be Christian.[5] In the case of Haiti, the 2010 earthquake was blamed on demons; with a call for Christians to increase spiritual warfare prayer.[6]

---

spiritual-warfare-1993

[3] Carl Moeller, "North Korea Spiritual Warfare: Insights from Carl Moeller", Christian Broadcasting Network, 12-3-2010

[4] Spiritual Warfare, https://en.wikipedia.org/wiki/Spiritual_warfare

[5]Ibid

[6]McAlister, Elizabeth "From Slave Revolt to a Blood Pact with Satan: The Evangelical Rewriting of Haitian History". Studies in Religion/Sciences (2012-04-25).

Spiritual warfare has become a prominent feature among Pentecostals from its early use in the Welch Revival, which had leaders like Evan Roberts and Jessie Penn- Lewis; who documented some concepts in her classic of 1912 *War on the Saints*; a book unsurpassed in its thoroughness in addressing the influence of evil spirits on a Christian. However, Jessie Penn-Lewis' writings, pose a very different kind of spiritual warfare than that proposed by the leaders of the third-wave Charismatic movement like C. Peter Wagner and Cindy Jacobs, who was involved in Strategic Level Spiritual Warfare.

Other Pentecostal and charismatic pastors, who have emphasized using the power of the blood of Christ in the deliverance ministry include, Don Basham, Derek Prince, Win Worley, Bishop Larry Gaiters, Dr. Marcus Haggard, and Missionary Norman Parish.[7] Pastor Pedro Okoro, the Award-winning and bestselling author of *The Ultimate Guide to Spiritual Warfare,* on the other hand, espouses the notion of fighting the enemy from victory, not for victory. He encourages Christians to stop struggling with the devil, and instead, start using their authority in Christ.

---

[7] https://en.wikipedia.org/wiki/Spiritual_warfare

2. *The Lausanne Covenant*

Spiritual warfare is necessary for the survival of the human race, and for a man to fulfill the purposes of God on earth, and at the same time snatching lost souls from the jaws of Satan.

This war is real and ongoing, and will only end when that old devil is cast into the Lake of Fire. We cannot fight him alone, not as one individual, but as the church, as a community, and as a nation, we surely can. However, our victory over him will be more significant, the more our numbers increase and the more united we are. This is not a new idea, our brothers of the Lausanne Committee for World Evangelization recognized this when 2,700 Christian religious leaders from over 150 countries were called by a committee headed by Billy Graham in 1974 to draft a Christian religious manifesto to promote active global Christian evangelism.

The drafting committee for this document was chaired by John Stott of the United Kingdom. The final *Lausanne Covenant* was adopted by 2,300 evangelicals at the International Congress on World Evangelization in Lausanne, Switzerland, from which it takes its name. The Lausanne Covenant [8] contained 15 statements of affirmation and resolve. Statement 12 has to do with Spiritual Conflict as quoted below:

---

[8] The Lausanne Covenant
https://www.lausanne.org/content/covenant/lausanne-covenant

Statement 12. Spiritual Conflict

"We believe that we are engaged in constant spiritual warfare with the principalities and powers of evil, who are seeking to overthrow the Church and frustrate its task of world evangelization. We know our need to equip ourselves with God's armor and to fight this battle with the spiritual weapons of truth and prayer. For we detect the activity of our enemy, not only in false ideologies outside the Church but also inside it, in false gospels which twist Scripture and put people in place of God. We need both watchfulness and discernment to safeguard the biblical gospel. We acknowledge that we ourselves are not immune to the worldliness of thoughts and action, that is, to surrender to secularism. For example, although careful studies of church growth, both numerical and spiritual, are right and valuable, we have sometimes neglected them. At other times, desirous of ensuring a response to the gospel, we have compromised our message, manipulated our hearers through pressure techniques, and become unduly preoccupied with statistics or even dishonest in our use of them. All this is worldly. The Church must be in the world; the world must not be of the Church".

(Eph. 6:12; II Cor. 4:3,4; Eph. 6:11,13-18; II Cor. 10:3-5; I John 2:18-26; 4:1-3; Gal. 1:6-9; II Cor. 2:17; 4:2; John 17:15)"

The Lausanne Covenant was followed by the Manila Manifesto in 1989 which stated thus:

"We affirm that spiritual warfare demands spiritual weapons and that we must both preach the word in the power of the Spirit, and pray constantly that we may enter into Christ's victory over the principalities and powers of evil."

This was later followed by the Statement on Spiritual Warfare in 1993. This statement, which I think is a significant document, is stated in its entirety below. It was used by permission.

Lausanne Committee for World Evangelization

Statement on Spiritual Warfare (1993)

A Working Group Report

"The Intercession Working Group (IWG) of the Lausanne Committee for World Evangelization met at Fairmile Court in London July 10-14, 1993. We discussed for one full day the subject of spiritual warfare. It had been noted at our IWG Prayer Leaders' Retreat at The Cove in North Carolina, USA, the previous November, that spiritual warfare was a subject of some concern in the evangelical world. The IWG asked its members to write papers reflecting on this emphasis in each of their regions and these papers formed the basis of our discussion.

We affirmed again statement 12 on "Spiritual Conflict" in The Lausanne Covenant:

"We believe that we are engaged in constant spiritual warfare with the principalities and powers of evil who are seeking to overthrow the church and frustrate its task of evangelization.

"We know our need to equip ourselves with God's armor and to fight this battle with the spiritual weapons of truth and prayer, for we detect the activity of our enemy, not only in false ideologies outside the church but also inside it, in false gospels which twist Scripture and put man in the place of God.

We need both watchfulness and discernment to safeguard the biblical gospel. We acknowledge that we ourselves are not immune to the worldliness of thought and actions, that is, to surrender to secularism..."

We agreed that evangelization is to bring people from darkness to light and from the power of Satan to God (Acts 26:17). This involves an inescapable element of spiritual warfare.

We asked ourselves why there had been almost an explosion of interest in this subject in the last 10 years. We noted that the Western church and the missionary movement from the West had seen the remarkable expansion of the church in other areas of the world without special emphasis being given to the subject of spiritual warfare.

Our members from Africa and Asia reminded us that in their context, the powers of darkness are very real and spiritual warfare is where they live all the time. Their families are still only one or two generations removed from a spiritist, animist or occultic heritage.

This led to a discussion of the effects of one generation on another. We noted that in the context of idolatry, the Bible speaks of the sins of the fathers being visited upon their descendants to the third and fourth generation.

Likewise, the blessing of God's love is shown to successive generations of those who love him and keep his laws. We wondered if the time we have had the gospel in the West has made us less conscious of the powers of darkness in recent centuries.

We noted, also that the influence of the enlightenment in our education, which traces everything to natural causes, has further dulled our consciousness of the powers of darkness.

In recent times, however, several things have changed:

Change in Initiatives: The initiative in evangelization is passing to churches in the developing world, and as people from the same background evangelize to their own people, dealing with the powers of darkness has become a natural way of thinking and working. This is especially true for the rapidly growing Pentecostal churches. This has begun to influence all missiological thinking.

Increased Interest in Eastern Religions: The spiritual bankruptcy of the West has opened up great interest in Eastern religions and drug cultures, and has brought a resurgence of the occult in the West.

Influx of Non-Christian Worldview: The massive migration of people from the Third World to the West brought a torrent of non-Christian worldviews and practices into our midst. Increasing mobility has also exposed developing countries to new fringe groups, cults, and Freemasonry.

Sensationalization of the Occult: The secular media has sensationalized and spread interest in these occult ideas and practices. This was marked by the screening of the film "The Exorcist." In the Christian world, the books by Frank Perretti and the spate of "How to..." books on power evangelism and spiritual warfare have reflected a similar trend.

Lausanne's Involvement in the Process: We in Lausanne have been part of the process, especially in the track on spiritual warfare at Lausanne II in Manila, and in the continuing life of that track under the aegis of the AD 2000 and beyond movement.

We recognize that this emphasis will be with us for the foreseeable future. Our concerns are written thus:

- To help our Lausanne constituency to stay firmly within the balanced biblical teaching on prayer.
- To provide clarity, reassurance, and encouragement to those whom the emphasis is causing confusion and anxiety.
- To harness what is biblical, Christ-exalting and culturally relevant in the new emphasis on the work of evangelization so that it yields lasting fruit.

We noted the following dangers and their antidotes:

Reverting to Pagan Worldviews: There is a danger that we revert to think and operate on pagan worldviews, or on an undiscerning application of Old Testament analogies that were, in fact, superseded in Jesus Christ. The antidote to this is the rigorous study of the whole Scripture, and always interpreting the Old Testament in the light of the New.

A Preoccupation with the Demonic: This can lead to avoiding personal responsibility for our actions. This is countered by an equal emphasis on "the world" and "the flesh" and the strong ethical teachings of the Bible.

A Preoccupation with the Powers of Darkness: This can exalt Satan and diminish Jesus in the focus of his people. This is cured by encouraging a Christ-centered and not an experience-centered spirituality or methodology.

The Tendency to Shift the Emphasis to "Power" and Away From "Truth": This tendency forgets that error, ignorance, and deception can only be countered clearly by biblical truth if consistently taught. This is equally, if not more important, than tackling bondage and possession by "power encounters."

It is the truth that sets us free, so the Word and the Spirit need to be kept in balance.

Emphasis on Technique and Methodology: We observed the tendency to emphasize technique and methodology in the practice of spiritual warfare, and the fear that when this is dominant it can become a substitute for the pursuit of holiness, and even of evangelism itself. To combat this, there should be no substitute for a continuous, strong, balanced and Spirit-guided teaching ministry in each church.

Growing Disillusionment: We had reports of growing disillusionment with the results of spiritual warfare in unrealized expectations, unmet predictions, and the sense of being marginalized if the language and practice of spiritual warfare are not adopted, and just general discomfort with too much triumphalist talk. The antidote to all of this is a return to the whole teaching of Jesus on prayer, especially to what he says about praying in secret that avoids ostentation.

Encountering the Powers of Darkness by the People Themselves: While recognizing that someone initially has to go to a people to introduce the gospel, we felt it was necessary always for encounter with the powers of darkness to be undertaken by Christian people within the culture, in a way that is sensitive in applying biblical truth to their context.

Caution Regarding Territorial Spirits Concept: We are cautious about the way in which the concept of territorial spirits is being used, and we look to our biblical scholars to shed more light on this recent development.

Warfare Language Can Lead to Adversarial Attitudes: We heard with concern of situations where warfare language was pushing Christians into adversarial attitudes with people, and where people of other faiths were interpreting this as the language of violence and political involvement.

We saw that the language of peace, penitence, and reconciliation must be as prominent in our speech and practice as any talk of warfare.

We are concerned that the subject and practice of spiritual warfare is proving divisive to evangelical Christians, and we pray that these thoughts of ours will help to combat this tendency. It is our deep prayer that the force for evangelization should not be fragmented and that our love should be strong enough to overcome these incipient divisions among us.

In his death and resurrection, Jesus triumphed over all the powers of darkness; believers share in that triumph. We would like to see evidence of this in our unity in prayer."

I have given the Lausanne Committee for World Evangelization Statement on Spiritual Warfare (1993) above because I would like to use it as a springboard to talk about the realities of spiritual warfare and how to use them to our advantage to gain victory.

So, the War is Real!

Spiritual warfare, as we have highlighted, is not an option; it is a reality. Satan's anger against the Lord has been transferred to the human race because he became jealous of the image of God in man. He was successful in getting Adam and Eve to join his rebellion against God by misleading them into doubting God's word and disobeying Him.

Now, as the children of Adam and Eve, we inherited their sinful nature, and as a result, we are born into this world alienated from God with the tendency to do evil. The Apostle Paul says that we are by nature, children of wrath (Eph. 2:3).

Furthermore, as Adam's children, we have suffered the result of his disobedience: sin brought misery, emotional and physical suffering, and finally death. There is only one way out of this sad situation; the way provided by God, through the sacrifice of Jesus on the cross, which frees us from the penalty of eternal death (Ro. 5:6-10).

Salvation and life are only possible through Jesus. He is the only way back to the relationship with God from which we have fallen. Jesus said, *"I am the way, the truth, and the life. No one comes to the Father except through Me" (Jn. 14:6)*. In the face of Satan's eternal condemnation, this has made his hate to boil over; the possibility of man's salvation and his glorious position in Christ in this world and in the world to come. Those who have restored the relationship with the Father through Jesus will have to face a barrage of daily insults and attacks from Satan, even though he knows he is defeated. He will do his best to deceive us as he did with Eve.

Those who neglect or oppose biblical truth will face similar attacks and be overcome by him because they do not trust in the Lord.

So, Christians who enjoy victory in Christ will have to wage war for themselves and for those who do not know how to do so and also, for those who are ignorant of the fact that a war is raging.

Nevertheless, as we get involved in spiritual warfare, we should guard against two possible extremes. One, over-emphasizing the things of Satan; when we see demons behind every negative situation and adversity, and two, under-emphasizing the things of Satan; when we don't want to talk about the devil or think about him.

Our true posture should be one of scriptural balance, which includes the reality of Satan and spiritual warfare, and the reality of Christ's victory over him. There are Satan and his demons, there is a need to assist and minister to people, but there is victory in Christ Jesus! It is from this standpoint that the subject of spiritual warfare is presented and it is my hope that you will be strengthened to fight victoriously as you read, digest and apply the contents of this book.

3.   Spiritual Warfare - Paul's Commands

In writing Ephesians 6:10-12, the Apostle Paul gives two commands, and a reason, that relates to spiritual warfare. He gives a *general command* in verse 10 and a *specific command* in verse 11.

The General Command

In the general command, *"be strong in the Lord,"* the Apostle Paul is saying that we must allow ourselves to be continually strengthened by the power of God that is already available to us by our position and relationship with Christ.

The same power that raised Christ from the dead now dwells in us. "And if the Spirit of him who raised Jesus from the dead is living in you, he who raised Christ from the dead will also give life to your mortal bodies because of his Spirit who lives in you." (Romans 8:11) If we get a bit deeper into this matter of spiritual strength, we become aware that in Strong's Concordance, 1743, endynamóō, "be strong," translates to "be strengthened or be empowered."[9]

The verb *"be strong"* is in the *present tense form*, representing the continuous need for this strength. Our need for the Lord's power is ongoing, for the battle rages on and we have to use spiritual energy to fight constantly. To *"be strong in the Lord,"* we have to be continuously energized by the Holy Spirit who empowers our lives.

There will not be an occasion in our walk in this life when we do not need the Lord's strength to move ahead successfully.

---

[9]Strong's Concordance, 1743. Endunamoó - "be strong"

So, there must be a continuous drawing down of the strength of Christ into our daily lives through various spiritual disciplines including prayer, fasting, meditation on God's word and speaking in tongues.

Observe further, the verb *"be strong"* is in the *passive mode.* This indicates that strength is supplied from a Source outside of our own lives; it is a power beyond our natural ability.

As the Psalmist David said, we must know that "My flesh and my heart may fail, but God is the strength of my heart and my portion forever." (Psalms 73:26)

Unlike David's dependence on God's strength to make it in life, the New Age Movement teaches that we all have the inner power to win.

The New Age focus is on self. Through various spiritual techniques, one looks within themselves to find their answers. It emphasizes the powers of the mind; teaching that we all have unlimited abilities within ourselves, and that to think of oneself as sinful is not correct, and only brings weakness. This idea is unbiblical. If we believe this error, we will undoubtedly fail in the war we fight because our mental premise is wrong. To *"be strong"* therefore means to be made secure through Christ's strength, not ours.

The verb *"be strong"* is in the *imperative mood*, indicating that personal responsibility is required in utilizing *"the strength of His might."* Therefore a father cannot draw upon and use the strength of Christ for his grown negligent child's sake, nor can a wife use it for her neglectful husband's sake.

Each must make their own portion from the Source of all strength. The power of God is made available to every person, but it must be appropriated to become useful. It is there for the taking, by the one who sees its necessity in their life.

If we do not appropriate the power of God's Holy Spirit in our lives individually, we will be powerless, and we will be no match for the enemy.

Appropriation is what makes us Victors in Christ!

As spiritual warriors, take a moment and appropriate *"the strength of His might"* in your life today; *"be strong"* the war is real!

The Specific Command

In the specific command of verse 11, Paul tells us how to stand: "*Put on the full armor of God.*" By this, Paul meant that we should stand, by continually and repeatedly putting on the spiritual protection God has provided for us as believers.

You will be bombarded by satanic strategies designed to destroy you, and render you ineffective in your Kingdom pursuits. Therefore, you must stand by the power of God while maintaining your position in Christ. Just as we must continuously draw down from the strength of Christ into our lives daily through various spiritual disciplines, we must acknowledge that it is our sole responsibility to "*Put on the full armor of God.*" Not a part of the armor but "*the full armor of God.*"

4. *Put on the Full Armor of God*

Putting on "the full armor of God" is putting "on the Lord Jesus Christ."
God's armor is far more than a protective covering; it is our source of victory; it is the very life of Jesus Christ Himself.
It is standing in the strength of *"Zoe,"* the very life of God: the life that Satan always battle against and will always lose too!

Paul wrote in his letter to the Romans " ...*put on the armor of light ... put ye on the Lord Jesus Christ." (Ro. 13:12-14)* When a Christian does this in spiritual warfare, Christ becomes his hiding place; Christ covers him! The darts of the devil will have to reach Christ first, and these darts cannot penetrate the covering of God.

When we put on Christ, we become successful in spiritual warfare, for Jesus said: "I am the vine; you are the branches if a man abides in Me and I in him, he will bear much fruit; apart from me you can do nothing." (Jn. 15:5) However, since living in oneness with Jesus means living in the safety of the armor of God, we can expect to share His peace as well as His struggles.

Remember,

God offers us His victory in the midst of trouble, not in the absence of challenges.

The Apostle Peter wrote: " *Beloved, think it not strange concerning the fiery trial which is to try you, as though some strange thing happened unto you: But rejoice, inasmuch as ye are partakers of Christ's sufferings; that, when his glory shall be revealed, ye may be glad also with exceeding joy."*(1 Pet. 4:12-13) So, putting on the armor does not necessarily mean that we will not suffer trials and pains.

Truly speaking, it is the committed Christians who face torture for their faith, not the weaklings. It is the warring ones that go through the fire, but continue to testify to the supernatural strength that enables them to endure unthinkable sufferings. They stand as one with Paul who declared *"Nay, in all these things we are more than conquerors through him that loved us. For I am persuaded, that neither death, nor life, nor angels, nor principalities, nor powers, nor things present, nor things to come, Nor height, nor depth, nor any other creature, shall be able to separate us from the love of God, which is in Christ Jesus our Lord."* (Ro. 8:37-39)

Parts of the Armor

The Apostle Paul wrote in Ephesians 6:10-18 *"Finally, my brethren, be strong in the Lord, and in the power of his might. Put on the whole armor of God, that ye may be able to stand against the wiles of the devil. For we wrestle not against flesh and blood, but against principalities, against powers, against the rulers of the darkness of this world, against spiritual wickedness in high places. Wherefore take unto you the whole armor of God, that ye may be able to withstand in the evil day, and having done all, to stand. Stand therefore, having your loins girt about with truth, and having on the breastplate of righteousness; And your feet shod with the preparation of the gospel of peace; Above all, taking the shield of faith, wherewith ye shall be able to quench all the fiery darts of the wicked. And take the helmet of salvation, and the sword of the Spirit, which is the word of God: Praying always with all prayer and supplication in the Spirit, and watching thereunto with all perseverance and supplication for all saints;"*

I believe when the Apostle Paul was writing this particular passage, he was thinking of a Roman soldier dressed in his full combat gear and using this as a visual example; he describes the Armor of God as both a defense and an offensive weapon.

In total, he describes six pieces that constitute the full armor: three of these were considered defensive weapons: helmet, breastplate and shield, two were considered offensive weapons: shoes and sword, and one considered neutral: the loin belt. But he did not stop there, unlike the Roman soldier's armor which was worn as a garment, the Armor of God or rather the believer's armor can be activated by *"all prayer and supplication in the Spirit, and watching... for all saints."* Wow! Our armor is alive! It is Christ in us standing ready to take on whatever challenge that comes along!

(1) Helmet of Salvation

In the ancient world, many other nations used helmets made of cloth wrappings, animal hides, bones, or hooves, etc. but the Romans had the most durable and protective headgear of all. Their helmets had chinstrap, visor, and came down to cover the back and sides of the neck to protect the major blood vessels and respiratory structures. The *legates;*[10] led legions and the *C*enturions, and were in charge for 'centuries' or cohorts were the officers. Their helmet had a ridge on top on which was mounted plumage or some sort of brush, depending on the rank.

The helmet had a lining of leather, softened for comfort and good fit; which was a bronze cast for the soldier, iron alloy for officers; a metal crest for the plume; and a chinstrap. The highest ranking officers had gold and silver alloy helmets for parade dress. The well-

---

[10] http://www.primaryhomeworkhelp.co.uk/romans/officers.html

designed helmet will protect the soldier from various angles of attack. It was specially designed to keep the wearer alive.

The soldier's helmet was of great importance during battle. It was for the protection of the head; the most important part of the body, which is the basis for all his actions. With the helmet in place, the Roman soldier could face his advisory boldly and battle fearlessly.

The head is the organ of thoughts. We will learn with more details, that the greatest battlefield takes place in our minds. This is the area that the enemy wants to attack the most, and his objective is to damage us mentally. He aims at the assurance of our salvation. Satan's greatest aim is to attack our personal security and stability in life as believers. He knows that if we fall here, we are done for, so from the very moment of our regenerative process, believers become the target of Satan and his demons.

The only thing that can provide the necessary stability in the face of this sinister organized attack on our souls is staying firmly grounded in the Word of God.

The Apostle Peter counsels *"Wherefore gird up the loins of your mind, be sober, and hope to the end for the grace that is to be brought unto you at the revelation of Jesus Christ;"* (1Pet. 1:13).

The Apostle Paul also gave some good advice in Philippians 4:8. *"Finally, brethren, whatsoever things are true, whatsoever things are honest, whatsoever things are just, whatsoever things are pure, whatsoever things are lovely, whatsoever things are of good report; if there be any virtue, and if there be any praise, think on these things."*

We must guard what we let run free in our minds because Satan is very subtle to use what we think to deceive us.

He has blinded the minds of the unbelievers, and he will do the same to the unsuspecting or careless Christian. We must, therefore, have clear minds to be able to discern at all times and in all situations. This comes by immersing ourselves in God's word and prayer, learning more about how to discern mental voices, and understanding imagination.

(2) Belt of Truth

The Roman soldier puts on a very wide waist belt, which was the holder for a lot of equipment. There were loops for the different swords, for darts, for ropes and a rations sack. When the legions conquered a city, the soldiers would empty out the ration sack to make room for gold, jewelry, and any other loot they picked up.

The belt was tied in several places to stay in place so that no matter how the soldier moved about, fell down, climbed hills, etc., the belt was always in place with weapons always ready. If the belt were not on straight, then everything would be out of place for the soldier. This would cut down his efficiency in battle and may even cost him his life.[11]

The need for the Lord's power in our lives is constant because the battle rages on. As the soldier had to put on his loin belt every day to keep his armor together, so also must we must apply the Word of God to our lives on a daily basis to maintain our defenses. In every occasion in our walk with the Lord, we will need to draw upon His strength in our lives daily, through various spiritual disciplines including the reading of and meditation on the word of God.

---

[11]http://christianmomthoughts.com/what-is-the-difference-between-absolute-and-relative-truth/

The belt is the first thing that the soldier puts on when he is dressing. In like manner we should apply the word of God early in the morning, to find the strength to stand through the day.

For the soldier, much of the weaponry and protection depended on the belt being in place properly. If we do not use the word of God as our belt of truth, we have no foundation on what to base our warfare with the enemy on.

The belt held things in place where they needed to be: the truth of God's word does the same for us.

What is Truth?

More than 2,000 years ago, Pontius Pilate, a Roman governor asked a wrongly accused prisoner who stood before him, *"What is truth?"* The prisoner; Jesus of Nazareth did not respond to Pilate's question during this encounter, because Pilate apparently walked away after asking the question and simply washed his hands of the ordeal. (Jn. 18:37-38).

But John recorded earlier in his gospel that Jesus said to Thomas: *"... I am the way, the truth, and the life: no man cometh unto the Father, but by me."(Jn. 14:6)* Also, just the night before He met with Pilate, Jesus offered a heartfelt prayer to His Father on behalf of His disciples, which included you and I. He said, *"Sanctify them through thy truth: thy word is truth." (Jn. 17:17).*

Earlier, Jesus said to his disciples, "If you abide in My word, you are My disciples indeed, and you shall know the truth, and the truth shall make you free" (Jn. 8:31-32).

Knowing the truth will free the disciples from deceptions, errors, and heresies: it will arm them to resist the devil.

On the other hand, rebuking the Pharisees who did not believe in Him, Jesus told them they were of their father the devil. Then He said, *"He was a murderer from the beginning, and abode not in the truth, because there is no truth in him. When he speaketh a lie, he speaketh of his own: for he is a liar, and the father of it."* (Jn. 8:44)

God is the source of truth through His Word. Jesus embodies truth, and he stands against that evil being who is dedicated to falsifying truth in every possible way in our world. To say that something is absolutely true means that it is independently true for all people, even if they do not know it or recognize it to be true.[12]

Jesus said to Thomas: *"... I am the way, the truth, and the life:..."*(*Jn. 14:6),* this is an absolute truth whether a person believes it or not. Later in this book worldviews of truth is discussed where further clarification is given.

In the world today many ask if truth is absolute or relative. This should not even be a topic for discussion, for the Scriptures said *"let God be true, but every man a liar; "(Romans 3:4)* However, this is the state of affairs in the pluralistic world we live in now. The concept of "truth is not absolute" originated from *"the father of lies."* Jesus is the Truth as is revealed in the Bible, through His character, His teachings, and His promises. He is the personification of truth. Therefore anything that does not agree with the Bible is false, error, deception or heresy.

Unlike the biblical understanding of absolute truth, found in the person of Christ, many philosophers and scientists today have embraced the concept that truth is relative, which means that what may be true today may be false tomorrow.

---

[12] Ibid

To say that something is relatively true means that it can be true for one person and not for another. [13]

Then, there are others who have chosen to embrace situation ethics as the answer to the question *"What is truth?"*

Situation ethics is defined as "a theory of ethics according to which moral rules are not absolutely binding but may be modified in the light of specific situations."[14]

In the spirit of relative truth, some say "All religions point to the same truth." However, a review of the major world religions will show that they contradict each other on major beliefs and claims, so they can't be entirely true at the same time, though each claims to be entirely true.

If we look at the concept of God, for example, we discover that in Christianity, Judaism, and Islam, they all believe in one God. So in this regard, they all contain an aspect of absolute truth. However, neither Judaism nor Islam believes that Jesus is God's only Begotten Son. Therefore, they both fail to give a full revelation of God as it is taught in the Word, which is central to Christianity's claim to absolute truth. So, we must put on the belt of truth and fight from the position of truth

Now, unlike the Roman soldier whose enemy was physical; flesh and blood, our enemies are evil deceptive spirits, who even sometimes may enter humans or animals to attack us.

However, they generally operate from the spirit realm (which is discussed later). They are always working against the truth, sometimes mixing truth with lies to deceive God's people. They will come against truth head-on sometimes, but most times try to strike

---

[13] Ibid
[14] Webster's New World College Dictionary

compromises to remain hidden even in church and kingdom related businesses.

So in spiritual warfare, we do not battle by sight but by faith.

We discipline ourselves daily by delving into God's word to increase our understanding of truth, and to become sensitive to the Spirit's leading, so we can wrestle from the position of truth, for the establishment of truth.

When the light of truth shines, the kingdom of darkness will fall.

(3) Breastplate of Righteousness

The Roman soldier's armor was designed to be lightweight, combined with ease of movement and protection from blows. The soldier had to put on his belt before he put on the breastplate because the breastplate which was attached to the belt by leather thongs passed through rings on the bottom to keep it solidly attached. The breastplate was anchored to the belt, and it was above the belt. The Soldier's breastplate protected his heart.

While the physical heart is the key organ responsible for sending blood through our circulatory system to keep us alive, our spiritual hearts keep our spiritual lives quickened as we maintain right relationships with God!

The Bible declares that the heart of man is prone to be tempted: "Watch and pray, that ye enter not into temptation: the spirit indeed is willing, but the flesh is weak." (Mt. 26:41).

Believers are righteous in God's sight because of what Jesus did for us on the cross.

We refer to this as the *imputed righteousness* of Christ. It's also called *positional righteousness* because it results from your position or standing in Christ.

2 Corinthians 5:21 says that God made Christ, *"who knew no sin to be sin on our behalf, that we might become the righteousness of God in Him."* Every believer is clothed in the garment of Christ's righteousness. You don't put that on. It's already yours in Christ.[15] When you got born-again, your Heavenly father put that robe on you.

However, there is *practical righteousness* which takes the place of *self-righteousness* in our lives after we are saved. When we were not saved, we used to have self-righteousness as deceived persons and thought "I can please God and reach heaven on my own merit." But now, we employ practical righteousness to our lives in our walk with Christ.

Practical Righteousness

Practical righteousness is moment-by-moment obedience to the Lord.

It involves the right thinking and right actions as we walk daily with the Lord.

Putting on the breastplate speaks of aligning our hearts with God's will. The heart speaks of practical sanctification through the imputed righteousness of Christ. It also represents the deep work of the Holy Spirit through Spirit-filled living without which, we leave ourselves open to the devil's attack.

---

[15]   http://www.erictyoung.com/2010/09/15/developing-practical-righteousness-%E2%80%94-john-macarthur/

Sin in our life is like a hole in our breastplate; it creates space for the enemy to work from: *"Keep thy heart with all diligence; for out of it are the issues of life."* (Pr. 4:23) However, when we walk in the righteousness of Christ, it is a weapon of defense against all those fiery darts, slanderous accusations, and outrageous strategies of the devil.

Backsliding from the heart is not an option for the believer just as it was not an option for the Roman soldier to turn his back on his enemy. His breastplate only covered the front. Turning their back on their enemy was always fatal. Overcoming the strong man is only possible when you face him.

Practical righteousness is closely related to the human side of progressive sanctification. It is true that God is the One who sanctifies the believer, but progressive sanctification requires the daily or momentary inputs from the Christian.

The Apostle Paul tells us, "For it is God that worketh in you both to will and do of his good pleasure" (Phil. 2:13). But we are also told to: "Sanctify yourselves, therefore, and be ye holy; for I am the Lord your God." (Lev. 20:7)

Before crossing the Nile, "Joshua said unto the people, Sanctify yourselves: for tomorrow the Lord will do wonders among you" (Josh. 3:5). Again the Apostle Paul tells us "Having, therefore, these promises, dearly beloved, let us cleanse ourselves from all filthiness of the flesh and spirit, perfecting holiness in the fear of God" (2 Cor. 7:1).

Walking in practical righteousness requires *walking by faith*. The Apostle Paul in recounting his salvation experience stated what the Lord told him as His purpose for coming to the earth; *"To open their eyes, and to turn them from darkness to light, and from the power of Satan unto God, that they may receive forgiveness of sins, and inheritance among them which are sanctified by faith that is in me."*

(Acts 26:18). Basically, Jesus told Paul I will save and deliver them, but thereafter they must walk by faith. It is by faith that the believer lays hold of the cleansing blood of Jesus Christ. On a daily basis, we must apply the blood on our hearts and have freedom from condemnation.

Practical righteousness also requires that we live in *obedience to the Word of God*, for Jesus said to His disciples: *"Now ye are clean through the word which I have spoken unto you."* (Jn. 15:3) Later, in His prayer for His disciples, He asked the Father to *"Sanctify them through thy truth: thy word is truth."* (Jn. 17:17)

In the same vein, the beloved disciple John said: "If we walk in the light, as he is in the light, we have fellowship one with another and the blood of Jesus Christ his Son cleanseth us from all sin" (1 Jn. 1:7). David, the psalmist said: "Thy word is a lamp unto my feet and a light unto my path" (Ps. 119:105).

Although God has provided His word, every successful Christian soldier will make it a habit of obeying God's word.

Furthermore, practical righteousness requires *yielding to the Holy Spirit.* Yielding is necessary because the Holy Spirit is Gentle: He does not force Himself on anyone. There must be a readiness to give oneself to controlling influence. As we do this, He gets the chance He needs to reveal Christ to us, bring greater illumination of God's word, baptize and fill us afresh, anoint us for service and guide us into the future: *"Howbeit when he, the Spirit of truth, is come, he will guide you into all truth: for he shall not speak of himself; but whatsoever he shall hear, that shall he speak: and he will shew you things to come"* (Jn. 16:13).

As mentioned earlier, there will not be an occasion in our walk with the Lord when we will not need His strength, so we must continuously draw from his strength, through the application of various spiritual principles.

Like the soldier who must put on the whole armor daily, *we must make a personal commitment to walk in righteousness*. Through personal commitment, we set ourselves apart for the war that we must fight.

In this regard, Paul counsels Timothy: "No man that warreth entangleth himself with the affairs of this life; that he may please him who hath chosen him to be a soldier."(2 Tim. 2:4) This can be difficult for some of us, but we must be ready to commit ourselves to practical righteousness, with the confidence that the Lord is walking with us in these difficult areas of our lives.

Personal commitment is not only required in the area of spiritual warfare, but also in the area of service. Deep down on the inside, we must say "Lord I will do what you want me to do and go where you want me to go!" This also is difficult, because it often takes you out of your comfort zone and exposes you to uncalculated challenges in life.

Only a pure heart covered by a breastplate of righteousness follows the Lord out of pure love: *"We love him because he first loved us."*(1 Jn. 4:19)

Knowing the difficulty, the Apostle Paul begs: "I beseech you, therefore, brethren, by the mercies of God, that ye present your bodies a living sacrifice, holy, acceptable unto God, which is your reasonable service. And be not conformed to this world: but be ye transformed by the renewing of your mind that ye may prove what is that good, and acceptable, and perfect will of God." (Ro. 12:1, 2)

(4) Shield of Faith

The shield of the Roman soldier was carried on his left side, it had a long, rectangular, knees-to-chin, semi-circular shape, which deflected arrows and spears and could be knelt behind during an arrow barrage. Groups of soldiers who were besieging a town could come close together and hold their shields over their heads to form a huge circle to protect the group from fiery arrows. This is a great picture of team dynamics in spiritual warfare.

Christian soldiers need to stay together, focus on the enemy while watching each other's backs at the same time.

The shield of faith represents the faith of a believer in the promises of God. The value of faith lies not in the person exercising it, but in the person whom the faith is in. However, the results of faith depend on the person exercising faith. Faith is not a stranger to the human race, because people exercise it daily every day in the natural world. Romans 10:17 tells us that faith comes by hearing and hearing by the Word of God. Having a relationship with God and searching the scriptures helps believers to develop greater faith for life, service and spiritual warfare.

As Christian soldiers, we must develop faith in our lives: it is our shield.

Developing faith is developing the principle of action and power for survival.

Faith takes us on the side of God: "But without faith, it is impossible to please him: for he that cometh to God must believe that he is and that he is a rewarder of them that diligently seek him." (Heb. 11:6). "Faith comes by hearing, and hearing by the Word of God." (Ro. 10:17).

Since it takes the Word of God to birth faith in our hearts, it will take the same Word of God to sustain faith in our lives: for "the just shall live by faith" (Heb. 2:4)

The Word of God strengthens our soul and gives us confidence in

God, resulting in courage for life, service, and power to fight.

The Word brings Faith

Christians live at various levels of faith: Sometimes we have *no faith* like the disciples who faced a difficult moment when they were caught in the storm. They cried out to Jesus who awoke and asked *"Why are ye so fearful? How is it that ye have no faith?"* (Mk. 4:40).

No faith represents a state of no confidence in the power and abilities of God.

Can a believer be in this state? Yes! It is noteworthy to observe that, in this crisis moment, all of the men in the boat were believers, but they had no faith. What people believe in crises is usually the minimum of what they believe in good times. These brothers' carelessness about the way they treated God's word in their lives was revealed here. They needed to know that a spiritual warlord must constantly feed on the word of God. Meditating on the word of God helps us to internalize God's message to us, and that builds our faith: *"Faith comes by hearing, and hearing by the Word of God."* (Ro. 10:17)

Generally, everyone seems to start their Christian life with some amount of faith. It may be called w*eak faith.*

Weak faith is the kind of faith that considers circumstances.

It is better than *no faith,* although it constantly limits the extent of the manifestation of God and His abilities. Sometimes bad theology and wrong teachings can contribute to weak faith. Thinking that the days of miracles are over and the operation of spiritual gifts ceased when the last apostle died, will not be helpful to one's faith development. This kind of belief hardly sees the Spirit moving, the power of God operating, or that God can do the impossible.

Some have *temporary faith* as they grow stronger.

Temporary faith receives the Word of God for a while, and believes, but fail when tests of life come.

Peter stepped down into the waters and said, *"Lord bid me come"(Mt. 14:28),* and Jesus said, *"come."* At that moment his self-talk probably went like this "I'm going to walk because the Lord said for me to walk," and he started walking on water. But when he got his eyes on the huge waves, he got scared and sank. It is like people who got healed but are looking at their symptoms and eventually fall sick back.

But others develop *active faith* because they allow the Word of God to take roots in their hearts.

"But that on the good ground are they, which in an honest and good heart, having heard the word, keep it, and bring forth fruit with patience."(Lu. 8:15) They understand that faith without works is dead (Jam. 2:14-26).

The Scriptures states that even the demons believe and tremble, so we need to do more than just believe in overcoming him. We must act! The apostles acted on their faith, preached the gospel, did good works and overcame the strong man, Satan.

Abraham "staggered not at the promise of God through unbelief; but was strong in faith, giving glory to God; "(Ro. 4:20). Like Abraham, those who continue to grow through God's word develop strong faith.

Strong faith does not stagger at God's promises. It refuses defeat and does not take no for an answer.

The Christian with strong faith can say to the devil *"The LORD rebuke you, Satan!"(Jude 1:9)* and releases the Spirit of God into action.

Like the centurion whose servant was sick, those who have *great faith* have great expectations, so that just hearing the word is enough for the request to be granted.

The centurion said, *"Say in a word, and my servant shall be healed."*(Luke 7:7) When Jesus heard these things, he marveled at him and said: *"I have not found so great faith, no, not in Israel."* (Lu. 7:9)

Paul writing to Timothy mentioned, *"The unfeigned faith"* that was in him, his grandmother Lois and his mother, Eunice.

Unfeigned faith is genuine faith; it knows no hypocrisy nor does it brag or put on a show.[16]

It is very childlike, trusting and innocent, and is well founded on the Word of God.

Jesus had *perfect faith*. He had it, and it comes because He was the Word.

Perfect faith speaks of absolute confidence in God's own Word and Being.

Jesus said, "If ye abide in me, and my words (which this Word) abides in you, then ask what you will, and it'll be done for you." (Jn. 15:7)

When we allow His words to abide in us, we become the word, and the word becomes us. In other words, we and the Word become inseparable. In that state, *"if ye say to this mountain, 'Be moved,' and don't doubt, but believe in what you've said, then you shall have what you said. When you pray, believe that you receive what you ask for, and you shall have it; it'll be given to you."(Mk. 11:23)* When we

---

[16] https://heavenawaits.wordpress.com/different-levels-of-faith-%E2%80%93-where-are-you/

have this kind of faith, time, space or anything else will never change our belief in what the word of God can do. You have spoken, and it is done, it is settled. Amen!

With his perfect faith, Jesus was very unusual, and the devil didn't stay around Him very long, because Jesus constantly put him in his place by using the word: *"It is written..."* By speaking the wor, Jesus was Master over all circumstances. Perfect faith masters all circumstance no matter what it is. I pray that we all may rise to this level and operate as our Lord did.

So, when we operate with faith, we simply have believed, and we proceed to do what the Lord reveals to us, no matter what the circumstance is. Perfect faith masters instead of considering them.

It was with perfect faith that the Lord walked into a room with a dead child and said *"Talitha cumi"* (*Mk 5:41)* and the child arose. O that we will have this kind of faith as we walk in life's circumstances, and as we reach the people at the altars of our churches. Lord help us!

We know that Jesus is God and that His perfect faith was focused on God's perfect Word, which opened up the possibility for Him to conquer every obstructing agent that He came in contact with. Death or sickness could not stand in the presence of the Lord. Flowing from Him were rivers of virtue, going out constantly and even saturating His garments. Some people supernaturally understood this, so they lay in His shadows just lingering in His divine presence. For some others, putting just their finger on His garment healed them.

Our Lord was walking in a world of perfect faith because He was the Word, and simple people loved it because they saw an opportunity to perfect their faith through His own. By His faith, in His Word, we, or rather He through us can conquer anything.

We need faith to live and to fight. As the soldier had to put his loin belt every day to keep his armor together, so also must we apply the Word of God to our lives on a daily basis, to maintain our faith defenses against the enemy.

(5) Sword of the Spirit

History reveals that the Romans had different swords: the Gladius, the Spatha, the Mainz Gladius, the Parazonium, the Pugio, and the Sica.[17]

The Gladius is one of the most widely recognized swords of any culture. These swords were in use between 4th century BC and 3rd Century AD. The Romans were highly skilled and disciplined men, so great weapons such as this sword were a must, especially for cavalrymen and infantrymen. The skills of these men and their advances in sword making techniques made the Roman sword a deadly weapon. These were the major factors behind a long and successful military reign.

The name of a person's sword was often etched into the blade; this was how a person's sword was identified. The Spatha sword was also popular in Paul's time. It was a little longer than the common gladius. Spatha was the primary sword of Roman cavalry. Spatha was a straight and long sword, measuring between 0.75 and 1 m (30 and 39 in). Spatha was used in Roman wars, and of course also in gladiator games. Spatha was adopted by barbarian tribes later and evolved into early medieval swords. The Viking swords originated from this sword.

The Sica was a short sword or large dagger with a blade about 16–18 inches long (40–45 cm), with a short, sharp point and a slight curvature. This distinctive shape was designed to get around the

---

[17]https://en.wikipedia.org/wiki/Category:Roman_swords

sides of an opponent's shield and stab or slash them in the back. [18]

Paul may have considered the battle ready features of the various Roman swords, and not necessarily any particular sword when he was writing to the Ephesians.

A two-edged sword with the curved point was dangerous because it could significantly damage the opponent. Not only was it intended to kill, but also to get around the sides of an opponent's shield and rip the enemy's insides to shreds.[19] It only needed to penetrate into the enemy's body, a depth of two to three inches to cause a mortal injury. Another advantage of this sword was that the soldier did not have to turn his sword around to inflict damage on the enemy; it cut in two directions. This was seen as a very deadly and powerful weapon.

With this in mind, Paul likened the Word of God to this awesome and powerful personal weapon. The writer of Hebrews 4:12 said: *"For the word of God is quick, and powerful, and sharper than any two-edged sword, piercing even to the dividing asunder of soul and spirit, and of the joints and marrow, and is a discerner of the thoughts and intents of the heart."* Let us learn to skillfully divide the word of God so that we may use it effectively to fight the enemy.

God speaks with ultimate authority in the universe. He spoke, and the universe came into being from nothing. When we speak God's word according to his will, there is no power in the universe that can withstand it!

---

[18] http://www.swordhistory.info/p=120
[19] http://www.christianarsenal.com/Christian_Arsenal/Full_Armor_of_God.html

(6) Feet Fitted with Steadiness and Readiness

The Apostle Paul, still speaking with his imagery of the dressed roman soldier, now gives attention to the necessary preparedness of his feet. He writes to his brethren whom he was outfitting for spiritual warfare: *"your feet shod with the preparation of the gospel of peace"* (Eph. 6:15).

The word *"preparation"* suggests two different meanings. The first meaning has the idea of *'steadiness.'* In this regard, Paul says we are to have our feet grounded firmly in the Gospel of Peace, that is; the Gospel brings peace of mind because it provides sure footing in an unstable world of slippery places and shifting sands.

The Roman Soldiers were equipped with footwear that had spikes on its soles, which gave them a strong enough stance and balance, and also gave them a superior posture in battle on hills and uneven terrain.[20]

Some historians credit the footwear, as one of the greatest reasons why the Roman Army was so victorious over its enemies. The Roman soldiers were popular throughout the ancient world for their ability to march long distances. Sometimes up to 30 km in five hours, then drop their pack, and go into battle.

This was due to intensive endurance training, and the "combat-sandals" which they wore. They were the precedent to the modern combat boot. Their heavy-lugged soles gave secure footing, and the tight weaving of heavy straps protected the feet and ankles.[21]

---

[20]Ibid
[21] Armed and Able to Stand

In ancient warfare, battles lost or won was dependent on the weight of the masses of men that were hurled against each other; the heavier men, with firmer footing, were likely to be the victors.[22]

When the Apostle Paul speaks of *"your feet shod with the preparation of the gospel of peace;" (Eph. 6:15)* he is making reference to a firm foundation, based on extensive preparation of allowing the peace of God to guard your heart.

In his *Expositions of Holy Scripture* Alexander MacLaren writes "This peace will help us to stand with our feet planted firmly on the Word of God and to stay there, unmoved by the devil's threats and lies. It will protect us when we walk through the rough places and keep us steady in the heat of a battle. It will keep our spiritual foes where they belong...under our feet. A calm heart makes a light foot; and he who is living at peace with God, and with all disturbances within hushed to rest, will, for one thing, be able to see what his duty is. He will see his way as far as is needful for the moment." [23]

The quiet heart will be able to focus its whole strength on its work. This is what troubled hearts are incapable of, because half their energy is taken up in steadying or quieting themselves, or is dissipated in going after a hundred other things. But when we are wholly engaged in quiet fellowship with Jesus Christ, we have the whole of our energy at our command and can fling ourselves wholly into our work for Him.[24]

The second meaning of *"preparation"* is *'readiness.'* In this regard, Paul was saying, like the Roman soldier, we are always to have our sandals on. That is, always be ready to proclaim the Gospel of peace throughout the world. In the Scriptures, sandals and feet speak of service. In this case, it will be gospel related service: the readiness

---

22 Ibid
23 http://biblehub.com/commentaries/maclaren/ephesians/
24 Ibid

to share the gospel. Romans 10:15 says *"How beautiful are the feet of them that preach the gospel of peace, and bring glad tidings of good things!"* Here is Paul quoting Isaiah 52:7, which gives a picture of the feet of people who are running to give the good news; telling others about the peace of God provided by the sacrifice of His Son. The message rings out the possibility of peace in every life because the battle is already won and *"God reigns!"*

The sandals may appear not as important as the breastplate or the sword, but they are, and in some sense even more important. It's amazing, if you hurt your arm or your shoulder, you can keep moving, functioning and even get out of a danger zone. However, if you hurt your feet, and you become incapacitated, it can have sad results for you in battle, hence the need for necessary preparation. You may be the strongest man alive and have the best sword in hand, with the best helmet on, but if you can't stand up, you are defeated already. The necessary footing considered here is the readiness to go all out for Jesus.

The *Expositor's Dictionary of Texts*[25] of Ephesians chapter six gives the following commentaries on the readiness suggested by verse 15:

"We must be *ready for service*. The believer is not saved by his works, but he is saved that he may work, and the genuineness of his new life is to be manifested by service. Now the possession of peace with God, much more the assurance of the possession of the peace of God within us, will give us readiness for the performance of the service, which is required of us by the will of God, and defined for us by the necessities of our own generation..."

"But in the second place, the Christian must always be *ready for sacrifice*, and the possession of the peace of God will give him that readiness. He is not to go out of his way seeking for a cross, for that

---

[25] The Expositor's Dictionary of Texts

would be to make himself a 'martyr by mistake'; but if, while moving on his appointed path of duty, he is confronted with a cross, then he is to take up that cross and humbly and bravely bear the suffering and sacrifice which it imposes, for Christ's sake..."

"The Christian should always be *ready for sorrow*, and the gospel of peace will give him that readiness. The believer does not escape sorrow in the world, and he ought to be ready for its coming...The Christian should be *ready for death*, and the gospel of peace will give him that readiness. That which we most of all need in the prospect of our leaving the world, is a readiness to go."

Now that we have discussed the various parts of the soldier's armor, we should be challenged to seek the Lord and become stronger in the many areas of our walk with him.

We must put on the Helmet of Salvation, which provides the necessary stability in the face of the sinister's organized attack on our souls. Wear the Belt of Truth, so we can ensure that the Lord's power in our lives is constant as the battle rages on. We will apply the absolute truth of the Word of God regularly, to find the strength to stand through the day.

Putting on the Breastplate of Righteousness clothes us in the garment of Christ's righteousness. When we safeguard our spiritual heart, our spiritual lives will be quickened as we maintain right relationships with God!

Using the Shield of Faith helps us to develop the principle of action and power for our survival. We understand now that the value of faith does not lie in our exercising it, but in the Lord whom we have faith in. And, as we use the Sword of the Spirit, we will learn to skillfully divide the word of God, so that we may use it effectively to fight the enemy.

Finally, our feet will be fitted with steadiness and readiness. We need to have our feet grounded firmly in the Gospel of Peace, which brings peace of mind because it provides sure footing in this unstable world. We will always be ready to proclaim the Gospel of peace throughout the world, and we will perform the service which is required of us by the will of God.

We know that putting on *"the full armor of God"* is putting *"on the Lord Jesus Christ."* We affirm that God's armor is far more than a protective covering; it is our source of victory; the very life of Jesus Christ in us. As we put on "the full armor of God," we will be standing in the strength of the "Zoe," the very life of God; the life that Satan always battles against and will always lose too!

5. Spiritual Warfare - Paul's One Reason

Having given a general command in Ephesians 6:10; to *"be strong in the Lord,"* the Apostle Paul explains that we must allow ourselves to be continually strengthened by the power of God, which is already made available to us by our position and relationship with Christ through salvation.

Through Paul's specific command to *"Put on the full armor of God"* (v 11), God is encouraging us to be completely prepared to face the oncoming enemy; Satan.

The great Apostle then proceeds to reveal the reason for making these two commands in verse 12: *"that you may be able to stand firm against the schemes of the devil."*

God wants us to know that our real struggle is a real battle to the death, not for a trophy or monetary reward.

Satan's primary objective is death!

Also, this wrestling is not against physical or material adversaries which include people, circumstances, organizations; it is fighting against a hierarchy of demonic forces led by Satan himself. This battle is in the spiritual realm, and it requires us to be disciplined, ready and to walk by faith.

Our Champion has already won the overall battle for us.

God's ground men must skillfully and successfully build beachheads in the enemy's territories to take back the lives the devil has taken, so that we may populate the kingdom of God and dominate the kingdom of darkness.

Not only are there commands and a reason for waging war against the kingdom of darkness, but there are also rewards for overcoming the strong man. These rewards will be discussed in a later Chapter.

6. Warfare Realities # 1 - The Spirit World can be Seen

There is a Spirit World which can't be seen with the physical eyes but is as real as this Physical World which we are generally aware of.

Our physical world is three dimensional. Everything that exists here occupies space and is defined by its height, length, and breath.

Here I use God's method to describe the physical world. The Bible said: *"In the beginning God created the heaven and the earth"* (Gen. 1:1). Basically, He uses earth as His focus and describes everything else from here outwards and upwards. I will do the same.

So our earth with the seas, the sky, animals, birds, fish, trees, people, and the things man has made is a part of the physical realm we call a solar system. Our solar system is made up of the sun and all the eight planets (including the earth), dwarf planets, moons, asteroids, meteoroids, comets, ice, rocks, artificial satellites, and space-faring vessels. In our solar system, living beings are only known to exist on earth.

There are billions of stars, and no one knows how many solar systems in existence, but several solar systems come together to form a galaxy. The Milky Way, which contains our solar system, is so large that it would take an object 100,000 years to cross it traveling at the speed of light.[26] But, it is difficult to estimate how many

---

[26] Elizabeth Howell, How Many Galaxies Are There? https://www.space.com/25303-how-many-galaxies-are-in-the-universe.html

galaxies exist throughout the universe, because of the limitation of the instruments of man. However, even though recent estimates among different experts vary, it is believed that there are between 100 billion and 200 billion galaxies. Wow! this is immense, and too much to wrap our minds around, but this is only a part of God's creation. Nevertheless, as humans, we can generally identify with this physical realm because we think in relation to space and time, so much so that we often assume, that is all that exists.

However, the truth is that, there is a spiritual world consisting of many more dimensions of reality beyond that which we can interact with, by just using our five senses. Our Lord Jesus operated beyond the dimensional capabilities of this natural world. He moved beyond space and time, and sometimes beyond the natural laws that keep the physical realm intact.

For example, when the disciples lives were at risk at sea, He came walking on water. *(Mat. 14:25-28)* But how does someone walk on water? He operated in a dimension beyond the physical realm. In this case, He did not require a solid surface to walk on, because He was suspending the effects of gravity on His body.

Later on, He foretold the future while He taught his disciples; he spoke of political, scientific and natural catastrophes occurring before He returns to earth. These prophecies more than 2000 years old are occurring now as end-time events. How is this possible? Well, He operates in a dimension beyond the physical realm. In this case, He related to time differently from us; He saw the past, present, and future all at once, but yet in sequence and with detailed precision. *(Mat. 24)*

The Lord moves in a multi-dimensional way, in the spiritual realm, even while living in the flesh. Hence, even though He was a single person with flesh and blood, He counseled His disciples *"For where two or three are gathered together in my name, there am I in the midst of them"(Mat. 18:20).* How is this possible? It didn't matter how many twos and threes gather, He is in their midst, *"by His Spirit."* That is how we can have vital fellowship with our Lord in thousands of congregations simultaneously today; He operates in a multidimensional way, through His Spirit.

Our Risen Lord even materializes and dematerializes His body as He walks through the wall of the house to greet His disciples. *(Lu. 24:36).* This was a fete beyond this natural physical world because He has authority from the Father to defy the principles and laws that govern this world. When confronting Pilate in John 18:36, He said: *"My kingdom is not of this world: if my kingdom were of this world, then would my servants fight, that I should not be delivered to the Jews: but now is my kingdom not from hence."* In other words, "I operate way beyond the structures that you, Pilate and the Jews, observe. I am not challenged by your authority in this physical world so I will not even deploy my forces, I will stay true to my purpose that has its origin in the spiritual realm, and I will go to the cross!"

There is a spiritual world, which we also call the spirit realm, which includes *Heaven*, where God and His angels dwell, *Hell*, where Satan and his demons operate from, and *a parallel space* were you, and I dwell in every day of our lives. We do not usually physically see or feel this realm, but we can interact in it *"in the spirit."*

As Christians, we need to embrace the worldview that sees the spiritual realms, operating over and alongside the physical realms. We need an awareness of the superior authority of God originating in the spiritual realms, but also operating in the physical realm. This will allow us to function effectively, as we live in both realms of the kingdom of God.

So, we live in a multi-dimensional universe in which the spiritual dimensions exist in parallel, and operate in continuity with our three-dimensional physical world. Most humans cannot see into the spiritual dimensions, so we can only observe the physical side of existence. However, events in our physical world are shaped by activities in the spiritual realm. When we look at the physical world in isolation, we miss much of what is happening in the universe.

Apostle John said "On the Lord's day I was in the Spirit, and I heard behind me a loud voice like a trumpet, [11]saying, "Write in a scroll what you see and send it to the seven churches: to Ephesus, Smyrna, Pergamum, Thyatira, Sardis, Philadelphia, and Laodicea."... (Rev. 1:10 -11) In the spirit, John became conscious of the voice of God, and he wrote what he heard to the seven churches of Asia.

Similarly, Isaiah became aware of this same realm and was literally connected with the spiritual world through a deep spiritual experience which he had when king Uzziah died. He reported his experience in Isaiah Chapter 6.

Isaiah was not taken physically to Heaven but *"in the spirit,"* he suddenly became conscious of the spirit realm, and he began to have a real experience with the Lord.

In this experience, Isaiah said he saw things: "I also saw the Lord sitting upon a throne, high and lifted up, and his train filled the temple."

He also felt things: "Then flew one of the seraphims unto me, having a live coal in his hand, which he had taken with the tongs from off the altar: [7]And he laid it upon my mouth, and said, Lo, this hath touched thy lips; and thine iniquity is taken away, and thy sin purged"

He heard God speak and had a conversation with Him: "Also I heard the voice of the Lord, saying, Whom shall I send, and who will go for us? Then said I, Here am I; send me."

In the spirit, Isaiah was literally translated into this fourth dimension and had experiences as real as his usual experiences in the physical world. All of his bodily senses and his mind were intact and were in full use during his experience.

Enoch, in Genesis chapter five and Elijah, in Second Kings chapter two, were completely translated into this same spirit realm hundreds of years apart and never returned to earth. But they will reappear on the earth in the last days, to complete their earthly tasks as witnesses before the Tribulation ends (Rev. 11: 3-12).

Acts chapter eight tells of how the Holy Spirit translated Philip into this same realm, but for a shorter period to facilitate his teaching of the Ethiopian Enoch so that he could understand the word of God.

For Christians, consciousness and contact with the spiritual world are necessary in order to successfully walk with God, and fulfill the mandate of God for us on earth.

The consciousness of the spiritual world is necessary for growth and sanctification, especially for successful spiritual warfare. Lack of this consciousness may result in growth delays and immaturity, which will hinder significant victories in spiritual warfare.

It must be noted, however, that not only godly people become aware and make a connection with the spirit realm, but ungodly and devilish people do so as well, though for different reasons and with different methods.

Hence, Saul in his backslidden state consulted the witch of Endor in First Samuel chapter twenty-eight. He said to her in verse 8 *" I pray thee, divine unto me by the familiar spirit, and bring me him up, whom I shall name unto thee."(v. 8) ..."And the woman said unto Saul, I saw gods ascending out of the earth. And he said unto her, What form is he of? And she said, An old man cometh up; and he is covered with a mantle."(V.13-14)* Yes! She saw into the spirit realm.

However, the witch of Endor was in communication with a different place or location, different from what Isaiah encountered.

It was the dark side of the spirit realm that the witch of Endor was interfacing with, the underworld! With her familiar spirits, she was able to peep into the underworld, the place of demons, and fulfill her evil needs.

A familiar spirit is a demonic spirit, in league with Satan, God gave a strong edict that they should not be consulted.

Nevertheless, the witch at Endor did communicate with a demon in the underworld: a demon who impersonated Samuel and who exposed Saul's masquerade to the witch. Saul in his backslidden state believed this lie, was deceived and later, died for dabbling in witchcraft. *"So Saul died for his transgression which he committed against the LORD, even against the word of the LORD, which he kept not, and also for asking counsel of one that had a familiar spirit, to inquire of it;"* (1 Chr. 10:13).

Similarly, the young lady who had the spirit of divination that followed Paul in the Book of Acts chapter sixteen was in constant contact with this spiritual underworld, until the missionaries cast the demon out of her.

In some way, we may say that these women's lives were naturally supernatural because they were in constant contact with the spirit realm through the wrong location (the kingdom of darkness), and through the wrong method; through communicating with demons.

As believers, our lives can be naturally supernatural if we keep constant contact with the Lord of the spirit realm.
As Christians, we must be conscious that we dwell around people like the witch of Endor, and the young lady that had the spirit of divination, in our society today; people who are sold out to the devil and are serious about fulfilling his wishes.

The only way we can break these strongholds is to become more aware, and involved in the invisible spiritual world where we can see, hear, feel and understand more of the Lord's Spirit, and His heavenly hosts and engage in warfare there!

If we allow the Holy Spirit to flow through us freely, and we keep communicating and communing with God, waging war in the realm of the spirit will become natural to us. The more we operate in this realm, the more the surprise factor of this warfare will be reduced.

Christianity and the New Age Movement

Christianity is different from the New Age Movement.

The New Age Movement is both a religious and social movement, which has a religious worldview that is foreign to Christianity.

The New Age Movement is a multi-focused, multi-faceted synthesis of several Far Eastern, mystical religions, including Hinduism, Buddhism, Taoism, and Western Occultism, adapted to and influenced by the materialistic culture of the West. [27]

The New Age Movement's main goal and purpose is to prepare the world to enter the coming "Age of Aquarius." Unlike the religions that it has its origin in, it is not a unified, traditional cult system of beliefs and practices. It has no official leader, headquarters, nor membership list, but instead is a network of groups working toward specific goals. One of its main goals is to bring to the forefront a one-world leader who is called "The Christ" or "Maitreya." [28]

---

[27] The New Age Movement,
http://www.watchman.org/profiles/pdf/newageprofile.pdf
[28] New Age or Old Occult?*- Biblical Discernment Ministries - Revised 11/01

"The Christ" promoted by the New Age movement is not the Jesus Christ of the Bible. Rather, it is a manifestation of the spirit of the anti- Christ. The New Age movement has gained significant influence, affecting almost every area of the culture and structure of society, even the church!

Because Satan is its founder, this movement expresses itself in many divergent and mutated forms, from the blatantly obvious to the subtle. It is the basis of Christian Science, Unity, and some forms of Witchcraft.

The New Age Movement also presents itself in secular forms, in various human potential seminars, transcendental meditation, some alternative holistic health practices, and certain curriculum in public and private schools as well.[29]

It is a revival of very ancient, divergent, religious rebellion against the Almighty God, like the form that occurred in Genesis 3:1-5. In its many expressions, it continues in the pattern of that rebellion. It questions God's word, His authority and benevolent rule (v. 1), disputes that death results from disobedience (v. 4), and claims that through the acquisition of secret or Gnostic wisdom, man can be enlightened and be "like God" (v. 5). [28]

The New Agers have been making various kinds of contact with the spirit realm, to keep up with the goal to promote the one-world leader who is called "The Christ" or "Maitreya."

However, a Christian's encounter with the spirit world is very different from a demonic New Age spirit encounter, in several ways.

---

[29] Ibid

First, the Christian's source of entrance into the spirit realm is *the Holy Spirit.*

In the case of the New Age, the entrance can be through one or many of multiple spirit sources other than the Holy Spirit.

Secondly, the Christian's goal for communicating through the spirit realm is to hear from the God of the Bible.

He is the Lord, "Which made heaven, and earth, the sea, and all that therein is: which keepeth truth forever: *7*Which executeth judgment for the oppressed: which giveth food to the hungry. The LORD looseth the prisoners: *8*The LORD openeth the eyes of the blind: the LORD raiseth them that are bowed down: the LORD loveth the righteous: *9*The LORD preserveth the strangers; he relieveth the fatherless and widow: but the way of the wicked he turneth upside down. *10*The LORD shall reign forever, even thy God, O Zion, unto all generations.(Ps. 146:6-10)

Our goal is to have a divine encounter with the Almighty. In the case of the New Age, it is basically to ensure spirit consciousness. But it can be many things, including communicating with the dark underworld.

Thirdly, the way a Christian enters into the realm of the spirit is by faith, through Biblical meditation with enlightened imagination.

Speaking in tongues also assists us in entering into the spirit world. "For he that speaks in an unknown tongue ... speaks unto God ... in the Spirit, he speaks mysteries" (1 Cor. 14:2)

On the other hand, the New Age folks use yoga, non- Biblical meditation, contacts with the dead through séance and several other non-biblical means to communicate with the dark side of the spirit world.

With this knowledge, we should be able to understand Apostle Paul better when he said: "For our struggle is not against flesh and blood, but against the rulers, against the powers, against the world forces of this darkness, against the spiritual forces of wickedness in the heavenly places."(Eph. 6:10-12).

Therefore, to wage war against the kingdom of darkness successfully, we must embrace the fact that an invisible world exists.

We must develop greater spiritual sensitivity so we can enter into this spirit realm by faith, *"in the Spirit,"* and defeat our enemy who operates primarily from this realm.

Developing Spiritual Sensitivity

As we mature, God expects us to develop our spiritual sensitivity, so we can see in the spirit realm by faith.
God will even open our natural eyes to see in the realm of the spirit. We see an example of this in the Old Testament in Second Kings when the Syrian army came as a great host to arrest Elisha. When his servant saw that with his natural eyes he said, *"Alas, my master! What shall we do?"* [16] *He said, "Do not be afraid, for those who are with us are more than those who are with them."* [17] *Then Elisha prayed and said, "O LORD, please open his eyes that he may see." So the LORD opened the eyes of the young man, and he saw, and behold, the mountain was full of horses and chariots of fire all around Elisha." (2 Kg. 6:15-19)*

What literally happened here is that God miraculously allowed the servant to see into the spirit realm that was usually invisible and generally unknown to him.

However, Elisha was fully aware of this realm. Successful spiritual warfare necessitates consciousness of the spirit world, and the ability to interact with it and establish the purposes of God for the moment.

Another example of this eye-opening experience is found in the New Testament, in the Book of Acts when Stephen was being stoned to death. *"55 But he, being full of the Holy Ghost, looked up steadfastly into heaven, and saw the glory of God, and Jesus standing on the right hand of God, 56 And said, Behold, I see the heavens opened, and the Son of man standing on the right hand of God."(Acts 7:54-56)* Here, the Lord opened the eyes of Stephen to strengthen him in the greatest battle he would face in this life; the battle for his own life.

"59 And they stoned Stephen, calling upon God, and saying, Lord Jesus, receive my spirit.60 And he kneeled down, and cried with a loud voice, Lord, lay not this sin to their charge. And when he had said this, he fell asleep."(Acts 7:59-60)

What a way to go home! Stephen saw Jesus while in his physical body, and when his heart stopped beating from the physical pains of the trauma he was experiencing, this brother continued to see the Lord in the spirit. He was physically dead but very alive. All of his senses were intact but not in a physical form. His spirit was completely alive in the realm of the spirit, where he was welcomed by the Lord. The spirit world became the new zone of his existence. Paul, who was present at this stoning, wrote: *"We are confident, I say, and would prefer to be away from the body and at home with the Lord."(2 Cor. 5:8)*

Before he died, Stephen's spiritual eyes were opened to the realm of the spirit, through his natural eyes. His physical body was now dead, but, with his spiritual body, he continued to commune with his Lord in the realm of the spirit.

7. Warfare Realities # 2 – Truth Wins

The world view of peace we embrace will determine the outcome of the war we fight.

There are more than six thousand distinct religions and philosophies in the world today. However, all these world religions and philosophies tend to break down into six major categories or worldviews. These six worldviews include all the dominant outlooks in the world today, in relation to truth.

They are:

1. **Naturalism**: The belief that everything in the world is a component or product of the physical things of nature. It teaches that truth is usually understood as scientific proof.

Naturalism proposed the motion that only the things which can be observed with the five senses are accepted as real or true.

Therefore, everything can be eventually explained using the various streams of sciences; like biology, chemistry, and physics.

Naturalism postulates that there is no such thing as the supernatural, including God, souls, and spirits. Therefore there is no place for supernatural revelation, angelic visitation, demon possession, and the likes. There is no free will, purpose or emotion, and there is no enduring self beyond physical death. The grave is man's end.

The scriptures, however, declares: "Through faith we understand that the worlds were framed by the word of God, so that things which are seen were not made of things which do appear." (Heb. 11:3) But, because naturalism denies the presence of an invisible world, and the impact it has on this natural world, those who embrace that worldview are already at a disadvantage in understanding and interpreting truth.

2. **Pantheism**: This teaches that truth is an experience of unity with "the oneness" of the universe. It explains that truth is beyond all rational description and that rational thought, as understood in the West cannot show reality.

Pantheism teaches that God is everything and everyone and that everyone and everything is God.

Therefore, you are God; I am God, a tree is God, the sky is God, a rock is God, an animal is God, and the sun is God. Hence, worshipping a rock or an animal would have just as much validity as worshipping God as an invisible and spiritual being because that object, in fact, is God.

The Bible is clear that the worship of anything other than the Almighty God is a sin.

It has consistently denounced idolatry which pantheism allows.

The Bible teaches of a personal God who is omnipresent: "Where can I go from your Spirit? Where can I flee from your presence? If I go up to the heavens, you are there; if I make my bed in the depths, you are there."(Ps. 139:7-8) God's omnipresence means He is present everywhere. There is no place in the universe where God is not present. However, this is different what pantheism teaches.

The Bible teaches that God is everywhere, but He is not everything.

People who believe in pantheism think and say God is the world around them. On the surface, this may sound good; however, what they mean is quite different from a biblical worldview of God and the world. What they mean is that everything around them is God, but that is not true.

The truth about this world is that even though God is present inside a tree, inside a boat, and inside a person, it does not mean that the tree, boat or person is God.

God is a being separate from His creation.

To effectively wage war against the powers of darkness, a Christian must be able to make a clear distinction between God, persons, and other things in this world.

If one does not embrace the personhood of God, he cannot effectively win the war against the kingdom of darkness. Remember, the worldview of truth we embrace will determine the outcome of the war we fight!

3. **Postmodernism:** A philosophy which teaches that absolute truth does not exist. It teaches truths as mental constructs, meaningful to individuals within a particular cultural paradigm. Truth is not absolute; they do not apply to other paradigms. Therefore, truth is relative to one's culture.

If taken to extremes, postmodernism will argue that what society says is illegal, such as drug use or murder, is not necessarily wrong for the individual.

Jim Leffel; a Christian apologist, and the director of *The Crossroads Project*, outlined the primary tenets of postmodernism in the following five points[30]

i. Reality is in the mind of the beholder. Reality is what's real to me, and I construct my own reality in my mind.

ii. People are not able to think independently because they are defined—"scripted," molded—by their culture.

iii. We cannot judge things in another culture or in another person's life, because our reality may be different from theirs. There is no possibility of "transcultural objectivity."

---

[30] http://christianity.about.com/od/glossary/a/Postmodernism.htm

iv. We are moving in the direction of progress, but are arrogantly dominating nature and threatening our future.

v. Nothing is ever proven, either by science, history, or any other discipline

Because Postmodernism rejects the existence of absolute truth, its adherents have no definite focus or destiny. They play right into the hands of Satan, *"the father of lies" (Jn. 8:44)*.

4. **Spiritism:** The belief in the existence of nonphysical beings, or spirits, that inhabit a spirit world.

In Spiritism people often try to contact spirits, which can include the spirits of the dead.

Like in the case of the New Age Movement, Spiritism makes contact for various reasons: to learn about the future, to influence the outcome of future events, and to gain knowledge. Through séances, mediums are used to make contacts with the spirit world.

They believe that the truth about the natural world is discovered through these shaman figures that have visions of what the gods and demons are doing, and how they feel.

However, even though the Bible affirms the existence of a spirit world comprised of both angelic and demonic forces, it forbids practices like Spiritism, because they open up people to demonic oppression.

Saul desired the witch at Endor to bring Samuel from the dead so he could get information about the future, but the Lord expressly forbade this in Deuteronomy 18:10-11, *"There shall not be found among you anyone who makes his son or his daughter pass through the fire, one who uses divination, one who practices witchcraft, or one who interprets omens, or a sorcerer, 11 or one who casts a spell, or a medium, or a spiritist, or one who calls up the dead."*

All witchcraft - like activities are malicious or ignorant attempts to gain truth from demonic creatures because there is no contact with the Lord.

But the truth about the future cannot be gotten through demons; nevertheless, spirits can recall information about the past. However, Scriptures forbid any such involvement. People, who depend on obtaining truth through Spiritism, will forever be in a disadvantaged position because Satan does not know the future, and he *"is the father of all lies."(Jn. 8:44)*

5. **Polytheism:** The belief that there are many gods. The Greek and Roman mythologies have gods like Zeus, Apollo, Aphrodite, Poseidon, and others. Hinduism has over 300 million gods of its own. However, in most polytheistic religions, one god usually reigns supreme over the other gods. In Greek/Roman mythology, Zeus is supreme while in Hinduism, Brahman is supreme.

The gods of polytheism are seen to possess characteristics relevant to human life, as their intervention in human affairs can be sought by rituals and sacrifices, or simply by their own will. Other than being conceived as immortal, such gods are often portrayed in similar likeness to humans in their personality traits, failings and vices, but with additional supernatural powers and abilities. Thus, they provided answers to questions of certain social, political and religious practices, and also helped men to understand the universe.

This, however, like Spiritism, exposes its adherents to a faulty source of information, and therefore fails in giving truth.

On the other hand, the Bible teaches that absolute truth is reality, that mankind is on earth for a purpose, and that eternal salvation is possible for those seeking a reconciled relationship with the one true God, in the name of Jesus!

6. **Theism:** This is the belief in one God as the creator and ruler of the universe, without rejection of revelation (distinguished from deism).[31] Theism teaches that truth about God is known through revelation. The truth about the material world is gained through revelation, through the five senses in conjunction with rational thought. The three major world religions have embraced different forms of theism.

In *classical theism*, God is described as having personal qualities such as goodness, love and other attributes that we can also find in human beings. It also teaches that we have the potential to develop these godly attributes, and also have the responsibility to do so.

Classical theism presents God as active within the natural world, rather than being detached from it.

It also puts great emphasis on humans experiencing God, who is the paragon of moral perfection, through symbolism, literature, and mysticism. Finally, classical theism conceives God in highly personal terms, which has come to fruition in the form of the human incarnation of Jesus Christ.

The Bible promotes theism. According to biblical theism, our God, who rules the entire world, is without a definite shape or form but takes on form as He wills. However, this does not make Him impersonal in nature. God encountered Moses through a burning bush and asked him to lead the Israelites out of bondage. When Moses asked God who he should say sent him, God replied, *"I am who I am." (Ex. 3.14)* He was probably suggesting to Moses, that He is far too immense and transcendent ever to be understood by man. However, as human history unfolded, Jesus, who is God incarnated in the flesh said: *"The one who looks at me is seeing the one who sent me."(Jn. 12:45)* The Bible reveals the fact that God

---

[31] http://www.dictionary.com/browse/theism.

communicates with human beings, and that He could be experienced in a very personal way.

Furthermore, Jesus said, *"I am the way and the truth and the life. No one comes to the Father except through me."(Jn. 14:6)* With this statement, our Lord was defining truth according to God. He is the personification of truth. Therefore, whatever is declared as truth must ultimately be defined in terms of God and His eternal glory. After all, Jesus is *"the brightness of [God's] glory and the express image of His person" (Heb. 1:3).*

Jesus is not only God incarnate in the flesh, but truth incarnate; He is the perfect expression of God, and therefore the absolute embodiment of all that is true.

From this standpoint, the truth is ontological. That is to say; it is the way things really are. Reality is what it is because God declared it and made it so. Light is light because God made it and declared it to be so *(Gen. 1:3),* and so is everything else. God is the author, source, governor, arbiter, ultimate standard, and final judge of all truth. [32]

Evaluating the Worldviews

On deeper inspection of these six worldviews, we find that they can be further grouped into two major worldviews in relation to the spiritual world.

The first major group implies that a spiritual world is non-existent and therefore unknowable. This group includes Naturalism and Postmodernism. They assert that anyone who is trying to gather truth from the unseen world is wasting time because truth belongs to this physical world and the experiences we can gather from our

---

[32] http://www.gty.org/resources/Articles/A379/What-Is-Truth?

five senses. Space, time, mass and energy explain the existence and functions of this physical world, and there are rational answers to all questions. However, the problem with this group that sees the world from this viewpoint is that they are hopeless in the real understanding of the world because they are only willing to accept the existence of one half of the world; the physical world.

Therefore, it is difficult for them to receive any positive impact of truth, in its fullness; into their minds about their future, because truth has its origin in God, and they are determined to reject the fact of His existence. They are destined to fail in life's greatest battle; the battle for their souls, because the worldview of truth we embrace will determine the outcome of the war we fight. These folks need to see the light. Apostle John said, *"But if we walk in the light, as he is in the light, we have fellowship with one another, and the blood of Jesus, his Son, purifies us from all sin."(1 Jn. 1:7)* Satan, *"The god of this age has blinded the minds of unbelievers, so that they cannot see the light of the gospel that displays the glory of Christ, who is the image of God."(2 Cor. 4:4)*. We must pray that the eyes of their understanding be opened, that they might see Christ and live!

The other group which includes Pantheism, Theism, Spiritism, and Polytheism believes that a spiritual world is existent and therefore knowable; that truth does not belong to this physical world, and the experiences we can gather from our five senses only. That space, time, mass and energy do not fully explain the existence and functions of this physical world, and there is not a rational answer to all questions about existence, because man's reasoning is limited. This group, which includes Christianity, sees that the understanding of truth may include various degrees of rational and mystic factors. Yes, mystic! Merriam-Webster Dictionary defines *mysticism as* "the belief that direct knowledge of God, spiritual truth, or ultimate reality can be attained through subjective experience (as intuition or insight)." Speaking in tongues can be considered as a subjective experience.

Christians understand that God created the universe, which comprises of a physical world and a spiritual world. We also believe that God, angels, demons and the human spirit live and can transcend across both of these worlds. So for us humans, to gather true information to do successful spiritual warfare, we must embrace a worldview of the origin and explanation of truth, and learn how to be more sensitive to both the physical and the spiritual world in which we live.

Christians believe God is the source of absolute truth. In fact, Jesus Christ proclaimed himself to be the Truth: *"I am the way and the truth and the life. No one comes to the Father except through me."* (John 14:6, NIV). Therefore, we believe Christ is Truth; hence, the truth is a Person!

Not only do postmodernists deny Christ's claim to be the truth, but they also dismiss His statement that he is the only way to heaven. Today Christianity is ridiculed as arrogant or intolerant by those who say there are "many paths to heaven." This view that all religions are equally valid is called pluralism.

In postmodernism, all religion, including Christianity, is reduced to the level of opinions. However, Christianity asserts that it is unique, in that it is the custodian of absolute truth. Christianity teaches that sin exists, that sin has consequences, and therefore, anyone ignoring those truths has to face those consequences according to the Bible.

The world view of peace we embrace will determine the outcome of the war we fight!

There will be winners and losers based on the worldview of truth, which they embrace. By no means will Naturalists and Postmodernists win the prevailing war against evil. They can only win, firstly, by expanding their concepts of the world to embrace both the physical and spiritual realm, and secondly, by embracing Christ as the source of truth. They have to believe that Jesus is the way the truth and the life. They have to believe that they are hopelessly lost! Like the lost coin of Luke chapter fifteen. They are not even conscious of their lost-ness, but, there is a loving Savior who is waiting to welcome them home.

The other group which includes the Pantheists, the Spiritists, and the Polytheists know that a spiritual world is existent and knowable, but they will also lose the war against evil because they refuse to embrace Jesus as Truth. The Scriptures clearly states: *"Salvation is found in no one else, for there is no other name under heaven given to mankind by which we must be saved."(Act 4:12)*

So, it boils down to Christianity as the only worldview of truth that makes it possible to win the war!

Even though the Bible as a collection of 66 books was written by over 40 different authors, with the time span of about 1500 years, between the earliest and last, the first five books though appear to have been compiled around 1400 BC, when science was almost nonexistent, the Bible makes some rather surprising claims regarding the nature of the universe and how it was created.

For example, the Bible says that God existed and was active before he created time: "In the beginning, God created the heavens and the earth." (Gen. 1:1) Paul said, "we speak of God's secret wisdom, a wisdom that has been hidden and that God destined for our glory before time began." (1 Cor. 2:7) From these two portions of scripture, we have some facts. Firstly, God existed before creation. Secondly, God created time "In the beginning (TIME)" before He created the universe "the heavens (SPACE) and the earth (MATTER)." Thirdly, the physical realm proceeded from the spiritual realm. "The universe was formed at God's command, so that what was seen was not made out of what was visible," (Heb. 11:3).

Fourthly, God commanded or spoke things into existence.

Because of the vastness and complexity of the physical world, made up of space and matter, science has always had difficulty comprehending its origin and structure. Thus, there has been several hypothesis and theories postulated to explain *"the heavens and the earth."*

In 1687 Isaac Newton discovered that gravity affects everything in the universe. The same force that pulls an apple down from a tree is the same force that keeps the earth moving around the sun. It was Albert Einstein in 1905 to 1915 who became famous for his theory of Relativity. He said that what we perceive as the force of gravity, in fact, arises from the curvature of space and time, and made some equations to calculate values. Around 1968 to 1970, three British astrophysicists; Stephen Hawking, George Ellis, and Roger Penrose extended the equations for general relativity developed by Albert Einstein, to include space and time, demonstrating that time began at the formation of the universe.[33] But God existed *"before time began!"* I believe God created time because it was His intention to create man who would have a complex brain and think linearly. Therefore, for Him to relate to man, time had to exist before man!

---

[33] James Porter Moreland, The Creation Hypothesis: Scientific Evidence for an Intelligent Designer, Intervarsity Press 1994.

8.   Warfare Realities # 3- Vision Affects Outcome

What we Imagine and See will determine the Outcome of the War We Fight.

Understanding Perception

When teaching the *Spiritual Mapping Seminars*, I would usually post several pictures to reinforce the importance of perception. The fact is that Pictures can deceive the brain. They provide distillations of objects or ideas into simpler known shapes.

Sometimes they create the impressions of representing that which cannot be presented in reality.

For example, you can see pictures of two persons walking at 90^0 to each other on the "same geometric plain" with one defying gravity by stepping on a vertical street, while the other is walking naturally on a horizontal street. It looks real, but it only happens in movies, not in reality! This is the trick of visual perception.

Depending on one's view and depth of perception, one may see different things in the picture of a single scene. For example, by looking at a single drawing, someone may see a pretty girl; someone else may see a witch, others may still see both and some people may see none.

 In the example to our left, one may see a pretty girl; someone else may see a man playing the trumpet, some others may see both while some may see none.

These are examples of natural visual perception. Once someone was shown the various possibilities, they will see these easily in the future.

2 King 4:9 is written thus: "And she said unto her husband, Behold now, I perceive that this is a holy man of God, which passeth by us continually." This is an example of spiritual perception.

Therefore, there are two types of perception; natural perception and spiritual perception.

Natural perception has to do with the physical senses and sensory organs, whereas spiritual perception has to do with the heart.

The Heart

Heart here does not refer to the physical organ in the chest that pumps blood around the body, but the spiritual center of a person. The heart is the eternal core of one's being that distinguishes one as God's crown creation, made in His image. (Gen. 1:26-27)

The heart is the center of hidden emotional, intellectual and moral thoughts and activities. *"Man looks at the outward appearance, but the Lord looks at the heart" (1 Sam 16:7)*. Jesus says that men's speech betrays the secrets of their hearts (Matt. 12:33-34) while Paul said that the mouth confesses what the heart trusts. (Rom 10:9) God knows our hearts (Luke 16:15) in its joy (Deut 28:47) and its sorrow (1 Sam 1:8); its raging (2 Kings 6:11) and its peace (Col 3:15); its troubled state (John 14:1) and when its rejoicing (1 Sam 2:1 ; Psalm 104:15); when it loves (Rom 5:5) and its selfish ambition (James 3:14); its modes of doubts (Mark 11:23) and of fear (Gen

42:28) and its mode of trusting (Prov 3:5); when it rises up in repulsive pride (Deut 8:14) or, as in the case of Jesus, is lowly and humble (Matt 11:29); and when one loses heart (Heb 12:3) or takes heart (John 16:33).

The heart is also the center of wishes, discernment, and desires. Moses said if we look for God with all our heart, we will find him (Deut 4:28-29). Jesus said, *"where your treasure is, there your heart will also be."* (Matt 6:21) As the eyes were meant to see and the ears to hear, the heart is expected to understand, discern, and give insight. But, understanding cannot be separated from morals. It is only with your spiritual heart that you can genuinely love and worship God, and this is why my praise and service mean nothing to Him unless it comes from my heart.

Both natural and spiritual perceptions are vitally necessary if we will go through life safely and successfully, both in our natural affairs and in our relationship with God. For simplicity, I discussed natural and spiritual perceptions separately. They are intertwined and most time occurs together, but they definitely affect each other.

Natural Perception

God made us with five physical senses which are controlled by our sense organs and brain: these form the basis for natural perception. Every day different stimuli around us will stimulate our sense organs. Many of these stimuli are received by our sense organs and are converted to sensations. These sensations are then transmitted to the relevant parts of our brains, which interpret them. Only after such interpretations can we understand what the stimuli are.

Therefore, in understanding the world around us, attention occurs first, followed by sensation and finally interpretation by the brain.

This process of the interpretation of stimulus is known as perception.

Natural perception involves two main processes: *sensation* and *interpretation.*

Generally, sensation for most of us will be the same unless we have some defect with our sensory organs. However, our interpretation of any stimulus is mainly dependent on the information we have gathered from our past experiences. Therefore, different individuals will receive the same stimulus, but will differently interpret on the basis of their past experiences. For this reason, a child who has never seen an iguana, either in a photograph or real life cannot identify the creature, whereas another child who has seen one earlier will locate it quickly.

Hence, perception may be defined as "a process of interpretation of a present stimulus by experience." [34]

Thus, persons who struggle with painful past experiences or abusive situations, have different ways of seeing the world and the people and things around them.

Sometimes hurting individuals will perceive danger, even when danger is absent. They have preconceived notions of what will happen and what their lives will become.

If you are not circumspect, they can make you fight demons that are not present, in the process of helping them to recover. As a matured spiritual person, you must be able to discern what you are dealing with.

---

[34] http://www.psychologydiscussion.net/perception/perception-meaning-definition-principles-and-factors-affecting-in-perception/634

On the other hand, there are others, who lack experience and are in danger but have no perception of the impending danger. Warn them! In this case, it is your perception (both natural and spiritual) that comes into play to assist someone from walking into a ditch. As a spiritual advisor, what you see will determine how others are helped.

Among the many things we should do for folks with poor perceptive abilities; leading them to Christ should be our highest priority, for in doing so their perception can change as they begin to receive victory and freedom from the problems of the past. *"Therefore, if anyone is in Christ, the new creation has come: The old has gone, the new is here!" (2 Cor. 5:17)*

Truly speaking, perception is not as simple as described above. It is an integrated process where different physiological and psychological processes are involved. The accuracy of one's sense organs, the clarity of sensations, the mental set of an individual, and other relevant factors can have a substantial impact on one's perception. Even If one of these is affected, our understanding may go wrong. Therefore we, as Christian workers, must pay paramount attention to our overall physical and psychological health, since these can have a significant impact on how we perceive the world around us. In like manner, we must take a person's general health into consideration when he or she describes things or situations he or she perceives to be negatively affecting their ability to live a well and normal life.

Also, as someone ages, the way their sensory organs give information about the world changes. Senses become less sharp, and this can make it harder for them to notice details. Because of this, a more considerable amount of stimulation is required before the individual becomes aware of a sensation. These changes can affect their lifestyle. They may have problems communicating, enjoying activities, and staying involved with people and these can lead to isolation.

Aging can affect all senses, but usually, hearing and vision are most affected. However, spectacles and hearing aids or lifestyle changes can improve one's ability to hear and see better and therefore; enhance their perception of the world.

WHO defines health as "a state of complete physical, mental and social well-being and not merely the absence of disease or infirmity."[35] I usually add "spiritual" to this definition to bring completeness to it. So my definition of health then becomes:

"Health is a state of complete physical, mental, spiritual and social well-being and not merely the absence of disease or infirmity."

Good health enhances perception!

Furthermore, several factors may contribute to individual differences in perceptual abilities, which may cause two persons to perceive the same stimulus differently. [36]

Through perceptual learning based on past experiences or any specialized training, every individual learns to emphasize some sensory inputs and to ignore others. Take medical doctors for example; they will be able to hear heart murmurs better than untrained people. In like manner, the trained eyes of some hunters will be able to more readily spot an iguana in a tree, than another pair of sophisticated, but untrained, eyes of an optician.

On the other hand, people with a defect in one sense may train themselves to improve their perception in another sense. So it is a common experience to see blind people who can identify others by their voice or by the sounds of their footsteps. Experience is the best teacher for such perceptual skills.

---

[35] Constitution of WHO: principles http://who.int/about/mission/en/
[36] Cognitive Psychology & Its Applications,
http://cranepsych.edublogs.org/files/2009/06/Factors_perception.pdf

With appropriate training, one may improve their perceptional abilities; they may see, hear and feel differently. So as Christian workers, we must tap into these possibilities to enhance our skills in ministry.

Our emotions and motives can have a substantial effect on perception. Sometimes a severe emotional disturbance can prevent perception completely, like when emotional shock causes individuals to lose sensation to limbs or their hearing temporarily. Or, in the case of hysteria, the individual can, for a short time lose several of their senses simultaneously.

Also, we are more likely to perceive those aspects of our environment that are related to our needs and our motivation, which can affect the perceived characteristics of objects. Therefore, hungry people see food items as larger as or more colorful than usual, and they can recognize food items more readily among other articles. Often their attention cannot be directed towards other things until their hunger is satisfied. This is why teaching or preaching to hungry people doesn't yield fruits.

Bruner & Goodman in 1947[37] showed how motivation might influence perception.

This team asked rich and poor children to estimate the sizes of coins. The poor children over-estimated the size of every coin more than the rich children. These are examples of distortion in perception associated with people in crisis. Challenged or hurting people often distort facts. Therefore, those of us involved in spiritual warfare must be aware that people's physical, emotional, mental and spiritual situations or crises may significantly affect what they perceive, what they explain and what they are requesting of us. Whether we pray that prayer or chase the demons, they speak of,

---

[37] CLASSIC: Bruner & Goodman - Value and Need as Organizing Factors in Perception (1947), Journal of Abnormal and Social Psychology, 42, 33-44.

must be dependent on what we see in them and their circumstances, and not based only on what they say. We should be specialists in this situation.

Another factor that affects the way people perceive the world is the way they receive and process information:

Every person has his or her way of understanding their environment and situations. As we know, there are four kinds of learners in the world, based on the way people receive and process information. They are visual, auditory, read-write, and kinesthetic learners. Many persons, however, perceive and learn using a variety of these methods, but one approach is usually predominant. Those who are flexible have excellent attention and are less affected by interfering influences. These persons are less dominated by internal needs and motives than people who are less flexible. Flexible people have less intrinsic issues in paying attention and learning.

The way people learn is usually the way they give attention to receive information. Therefore to obtain maximum impact from the world around you, you should train yourself to receive information in different ways. This is an educational skill enhancement that can yield great spiritual benefits.

When you enter a situation of learning, assess the method that is used and tune in to the flow of the Holy Spirit for that method. In this way, your preparedness is optimized, and the impact on your life will be enhanced. Move from the head to the heart, and learn to use the language of the heart to perceive what God wants you to hear.

However, in the work of spiritual warfare, you will encounter many persons who will explain their experiences, and receive instructions from you or the Lord, based on their predominant learning style. As you become aware of their learning style, you will need to adjust your method of impact to get through to them.

Learning the characteristics of the various kinds of learners can help you to discern who you are relating to:

a) *Visual learners* learn by seeing and visualizing things. They tend to be fast talkers, exhibit impatience and tend to interrupt when someone is telling their story. In their descriptions and explanations, they use words and phrases that evoke visual images. So, in relating to them, you should include demonstrations, like drawing figures in the air, or setting up small skits. Presenting visually pleasing materials such as drawings, diagrams or powerpoints would be also helpful to these individuals. All of these efforts are done with the intent to paint mental pictures for these learners.

b) *Auditory learners* learn by listening and verbalizing. They speak slowly and tend to be natural listeners. They prefer to have things explained to them verbally rather than to read a book. Because they think linearly, they process information as they are heard. In relating to them, as your strategy, you should sound good and should be planned; your speech should always be delivered in the form of an analytically organized conversation.

c) *Read-write learners* enjoy reading and writing in all forms. They prefer information to be given in writing. They learn by underlining texts as they read, by silently reading or rewriting their notes repeatedly, or by writing out in their own words the ideas and principles that were taught or discussed. They learn by organizing lists, diagrams, graphs, other visual depictions into ideal statements. In relating with them, your strategy should include writing out keywords in list form and putting responses, actions, diagrams, charts, and flowcharts into words. Also, they like multiple-choice tests.

d) *Kinesthetic learners* assimilate information by doing and solving real-life problems. They tend to be the slowest speakers of all and are reluctant to make decisions. They use all five senses to engage in learning, and they like hands-on approaches to things and learn through trial and error. In relating with them, your strategy should include hands-on demonstrations and case examples to be discussed and solved.[38]

Therefore, in dealing with the natural perception of different kinds of individuals, we have to improve our abilities to distinguish between their learning styles and modify our approaches to ministry in the area of communication.

We will also decide what level of trust to exercise in the information they share, and what mode of therapy to offer as we seek to heal their wounds.

Spiritual Perception

Natural perception comes from our five senses through learning and experience. But, is there any way of knowing about the world in which information is not derived from, by the use of our five senses? The answer is, yes! However, there are godly and ungodly ways of achieving this goal.

Some people believe in Extrasensory Perception (ESP) and have reported that they have experienced some perceptions without the aid of their physical sense organs. They call this the sixth sense, and it is the basis for clairvoyance, telepathy, meeting the souls,

---

[38] How To Teach Effectively,
http://lyceumbooks.com/pdf/howtoteacheffectively_
typesoflearners.pdf

precognition, psychokinesis, reincarnation, etc. These are all devilish means of tapping into information from the spirit realm on the side of the dark underworld. Scary, isn't it? Every Christian who will be involved in power ministry and power encounters must be aware of this.

Thank God, we Christians do not need this kind of sixth sense; we have the Holy Spirit, the Executive of the Godhead. The ability to see beyond our five senses is not found deep within ourselves or through communicating with demons, but through our fellowship with the Holy Spirit.
Spiritual perception, therefore, is knowledge which comes from the Holy Spirit.

We need both natural and spiritual perception to go through life successfully. However, we must make the appropriate choice when various occasions present themselves so that we can have maximum understanding at all times. We can choose to walk with natural perception or walk with spiritual perception. The well-experienced fisherman, Peter, and his partners fished all night and caught nothing. Peter knew the fish, he knew the sea, he knew the skills and even the seasons, but his profit was poor. Spiritually perceptive Jesus came to the scene and told the discouraged group of seasoned fishermen to go back out again in their boats. As led by the Spirit, He instructed them to throw their net on the right side of the boat and make a haul. The rest is history!

In life, he who perceives will receive!

In Luke chapter seven has the account of a sinful woman who followed Jesus Christ to the Pharisee's house. As the host Simon, the Pharisee, did not provide water to wash the Lord's feet, as was customary, this woman washed the feet of Jesus with her tears and wiped them with the hair of her head. She also took a flask of fragrant oil and anointed his feet with it. When Simon saw this, he said to himself, *"This man, if He were a prophet, would know who and what manner of woman this is who is touching him, for she is a sinner."* (v39) Simon's perception was guided by his social and religious past. He thought that he saw things the right way and that his judgments of people and situations were correct. He even judged Jesus as a non-prophet because he felt Jesus lacked appropriate perception of the people around Him. Jesus perceived the evil thoughts of the Pharisee and rebuked him for his judgmental spirit.

Jesus was different spiritually; He knew *"what manner of woman"* was anointing and washing His feet. He perceived her by the Spirit, and He saw that she was reaching out to Him, her heart desired forgiveness from the sins which she had committed. He felt the soul connection and said to the woman, *"Your sins are forgiven. Your faith has saved you.... Go in peace."* (vv. 48-50)

One of the things we must be careful with during spiritual counseling is listening to a person's story from someone else. The information must be weighed appropriately because it is not a person's past that matters but his heart; how it is placed on God at the moment of counseling. If we successfully deal with the person's heart at that moment of counseling, his future may become glorious!

Very often in the Bible, God asks people to be prepared for a special event about to happen in their lives. I see preparedness in Mathew 25:1-13, in the parable of the ten virgins who went to wait for the bridegroom. Five virgins brought extra oil because they were alert; the other five went wandering and lost their chance to be at the marriage. It is essential to be prepared at all times.

Proverbs 27:12 says "A prudent person foresees the danger ahead and takes precautions. The simpleton goes blindly on and suffers the consequences." While in Exodus 14:13 Moses answered the people thus: "Do not be afraid. Stand firm and you will see the deliverance the LORD will bring you today. The Egyptians you see today you will never see again."

Our mental preparedness or readiness to see, hear, feel or smell or taste some sensory input, makes us more alert and increases the possibility that we will have an expected spiritual experience. Such expectancy keeps persons prepared with proper attention and concentration. For example, when we are awaiting the arrival of a visitor, we listen for the honk of their car horn or their call at the door, even if there is a lot of noise around. Anticipation and expectation heighten our perceptive abilities.

In like manner, Biblical meditation makes us ready to allow the emphasis of some sensory inputs and to ignore others. As we give attention and concentration to the word of God, we can shut out both the internal and external noises in our lives. That kind of preparedness also assists us in distinguishing between the various voices, which may want to present themselves before us when we are trying to hear from the Lord. Jesus said, *"My sheep listen to my voice; I know them, and they follow me."* (John 10:27)

Spiritual Perception and the Voice of God

As we develop our spiritual perception, we will find it much easier to tune in and hear the voice of the Holy Spirit. After Elijah's high victory over the prophets of Balall, Jezebel sent a message to him that *"by this time tomorrow I do not make your life like that of one of them."* (1 King 19:2) Suddenly, fear and depression took hold of Elijah that he complained *"I have had enough, Lord,"* ... *"Take my life; I am no better than my ancestors."* (V.4) God knew that it was exhaustion and hunger that had taken over Elijah; it was his present physical status that was manifesting as negative psychological overtures. God knew that this soldier needed some TLC – tender loving care- before He could get through to him spiritually. So the Lord got His angel to repeatedly provide food for Elijah, which strengthened him for a forty days journey. This story teaches us that sometimes good people find themselves in vulnerable places in life by doing good things. In their valley experiences, they are like troubled babies needing to be nurtured back to life. This is where we, "God's servants," step in. We are agents of change; we help God's people get back on their feet!

Note, in the midst of his struggles, Elijah was maintaining spiritual perception; he heard and responded to the angel's command to *"Get up and eat, for the journey is too much for you" (v.7),* and he responded appropriately. Forty days later, after resting in a cave, *"the Lord came to him: "What are you doing here, Elijah?"(v.9)* His answer was basically, "I'm trying to save my life." Then *"The Lord said, "Go out and stand on the mountain in the presence of the Lord, for the Lord is about to pass by."(v.11)* Elijah responded, and God detailed to him of his future mission in the lives of two future kings and a prophet. *(vv. 15-16)* From this experience, Elijah described the voice of God as a still, small voice *(v.12).*

Habakkuk knew the voice of God (Hab. 2:2). Isaiah knew the voice of God (Isa 6:1-6). Moses knew the voice of God. The high priest Eli knew the voice of God (1 Sam. 3) David heard God speak and he, in turn, talked to God! (Psalm 60:6) God spoke to Saul on the road to Damascus: *"...Suddenly there shined round about him a light from heaven: And he fell to the earth and heard a voice saying unto him, Saul, Saul, why persecutest thou me?" (Acts 9:3-4).* For the rest of his life, Paul testified, "I heard His voice." (Acts 26:14-16). Peter heard and obeyed the voice of God. In prayer, he heard God speak: *"And I heard a voice saying unto me, Arise, Peter; slay and eat. But I said, Not so, Lord...But the voice answered me again from heaven... And this was done three times..." (Acts 11:7-10).*

Jesus calls the church at Laodicea to hear His voice and open up to Him: "Behold, I stand at the door, and knock: if any man hear my voice, and open the door, I will come in to him and will sup with him, and he with me" (Revelation 3:20). Successful spiritual warfare is entirely dependent on hearing the voice of God. If spiritual perception is poor, hearing from God will be problematic.

To me, God usually speaks with an inner audible voice. We perceive God's voice at the spiritual level of communication. Our spiritual eyes and ears must be in tune with the Spirit of God. When we are filled with Him, the Holy Spirit can communicate with the Father with *"groanings which cannot be uttered"* (Rom. 8:26) As He does, this revelations begin to flow, first as spontaneous words, then thoughts, followed by impressions and emotions and then visions or complete scenes.

These thoughts prompted by the Holy Spirit must be carefully discerned so that flow can begin. This is where waiting on the Lord becomes essential. The Holy Spirit will drop a word or a name, for example, and would expect a perceptive heart to pick up the signal that He wants to intervene or deal with a particular situation.

The Hebrew word used for intercession is "paga." Strong's #6293 give the following meanings "to impinge, by accident or violence, or (figuratively) by importunity:--come (betwixt), cause to entreat, fall (upon), make intercession, intercessor, intreat, lay, light (upon), meet (together), pray, reach, run."

Often, when the voice of God comes to us, it is like an accidental intersecting of God's thoughts within our minds. The Holy Spirit is faithful to His people, but He does not force His way into our lives. We may hear something in our spirits and see something in our minds that we did not reason in our hearts. This may be a chance encounter (paga). If we are discerning spiritual workers, this chance encounter can become the beginning of a power encounter.

Here, spiritual perception is essential again, because Satan may also throw thoughts in the battleground of our minds. Therefore, we must be able to make clear distinctions of what is of God and what is not. God's thoughts are always in line with His Word and His character. The thoughts of God are pure, peaceable, gentle, reasonable and full of mercy. They edify, exhort, bring hope and comfort. (James 3:17). On the other hand, Satan's thoughts bring jealousy and selfish ambition. They destroy, condemn and bring despair and are filled with rejection, fear, doubt, unbelief, and misery. (James 3:14, 15)

So, perception and spiritual maturity go hand- in- hand to make strong spiritual warriors.

9. Spiritual Warfare and Imagination

Spiritual warfare starts in our minds. Our imagination dramatically determines the outcome of each bout of our fight.

The Apostle Paul said in 2 Corinthians 10:3-5 "*For though we walk in the flesh, we do not war after the flesh: (For the weapons of our warfare are not carnal, but mighty through God to the pulling down of strong holds;) Casting down imaginations, and every high thing that exalteth itself against the knowledge of God, and bringing into captivity every thought to the obedience of Christ;*". Satan has dominated and distorted the mental faculties of man through sin, and he uses these factors as a means to win the so-called invisible war against man. He projects thoughts and imaginations to work against us.

Even after we get saved, if allowed, he can dominate and distort our mental faculties. He can manipulate us by encouraging faulty imaginations and thoughts that are disobedient to the word of God. And if we give way to these, they can cause us to be losers even if we never told another lie, stole again or committed any other sin.

Spiritual warfare starts in the mind so we must learn to be "*Casting down imaginations, and every high thing that exalteth itself against the knowledge of God, and bringing into captivity every thought to the obedience of Christ.*" Failure here can be deadly and have eternal consequences.

The Merriam-Webster Dictionary's definition of imagination is "...the ability to form a picture in your mind of something that you have not seen or experienced, the ability to think of new things, something that only exists or happens in your mind."[39]

To me, this definition engulfs three aspects of imagination;
1) The ability to create a picture of something unreal,
2) The ability to picture something real that you have not seen or experienced and
3) The ability to create a new picture of something that does not literally exist presently.

I think that Satan's mode of operation includes presenting to us distorted images of things belonging to the spiritual world, to draw us away from God and towards himself. He also gives such a bleak picture of our future that de-motivates us, or "takes the fight out of us," this is how he wins. These are the imaginations that must be cast down, and the thoughts that are to be brought under subjection to Christ.

But, there are also good imaginations. The Spirit of God can brood over our minds, and bring about a transformation that can cause us to be winners. In this regard, the Apostle Paul commands us in Romans 12:2 *"And be not conformed to this world: but be ye transformed by the renewing of your mind, that ye may prove what is that good, and acceptable, and perfect, will of God."*

Now, in the natural world, we are accustomed to trusting our senses to tell us what is true. What we see, hear, smell, taste, and touch are registered by our brains as truth to us. What we experience through our physical senses and our minds is held as truth. Like Thomas, we think that only what we have perceived, and can perceive with our senses can be trusted. On the surface, this may appear ok. However, if we continue to operate at this level, we will be restricting our lives to only the one side of our brain that primarily deals with intelligence; our left brain.

---

[39] https://www.merriam-webster.com/dictionary/imagination

MailOnline of 11 April 2012 reported that a team of US Researchers found the critical areas of the brain for intelligence were the following: the left prefrontal cortex (behind the left side of the forehead), left temporal cortex (behind the left ear) and left parietal cortex (at the top rear of the left side of the head) and in the areas that connect them. Intelligence is related to the left side of our brains.

On the other hand, the right side of the brain is responsible for imagination and creative abilities. Satan knows this, so he keeps us busy concentrating on left-brain activities, to take away our life of good and godly imaginative skills that allows us to see beyond this world. He can get us to be involved with all kinds of research, in the name of studying the Bible, in a bid to get us to neglect meditating on God's word; he will win if we allow him to.

Biblical Meditation is an imaginative process, which happens in the right brain. Meditation has to do with our heart more than our minds. When we meditate, we can hear the voice of God, and faith will arise in our souls.

God is calling us to present our minds and our hearts to Him so that He can fill and flow through both. Only as we yield ourselves fully to him, will we have complete life experiences, which will encompass both the physical and spiritual worlds.

Biblical meditation incorporates both Spirit-led reasoning and heartfelt revelation. Jesus allowed this divine initiative to guide both His heart and His mind as we see in John 5:19 " *Then answered Jesus and said unto them, Verily, verily, I say unto you, The Son can do nothing of himself, but what he seeth the Father do: for what things soever he doeth, these also doeth the Son likewise.".* So, let us seek to do the same. Let us do what we see the Father doing. This becomes an important tool in spiritual encounters and warfare.

Understanding Imagery and Imagination

Understanding what imagination is and how it functions, is very important for success in the Christian's life and to the development of a warfare mentality.

Basically, your mind acts like a screen on which images can be projected on, by one of three projection sources; Satan, yourself, or the Holy Spirit who dwells in the heart of the Christian.

Firstly, you are to discern and to cut off all pictures instantly put before your mind's eye by Satan. *"Resist the devil, and he will flee from you."(Jam. 4:7)* Secondly, for those pictures that originate from within yourself, you are to present the eyes of your heart to the Lord to fill with His thoughts, ideas, and pictures. By doing this, you will prepare your mind to receive from the Lord. This is where Biblical meditation comes in. It prepares the heart to receive from the Spirit of God. Thirdly, you need to discern and follow the images that are projected on your mind by the Spirit of God. Give them attention, space and time and allow the flow to take place. *"Today, if you hear his voice, do not harden your hearts as you did in the rebellion."(Heb. 3:15)*

If we give attention to the thoughts that are projected on our minds by the Spirit of God, cumulatively, they become pictures. And if we continue to wait on the Lord patiently, the series of pictures can become a vision. As we learn to wait, we will experience what our Lord was referring to when He said in John 5:19 *" ... Verily, verily, I say unto you, The Son can do nothing of himself, but what he seeth the Father do: for what things soever he doeth, these also doeth the Son likewise.".*

Jesus took the time to see the Father's actions and followed the instructions. He received these, as pictures created in His mind's eyes. meditating on the Bible allows us to practice this process, which, if we develop appropriately, will eventually become second nature to us, as we function in whatever calling God has for our lives. As we have conversations, preach, teach, intercede, counsel others, engage in spiritual warfare, etc. we must discern the origin of our thoughts and imaginations, and apply appropriate biblical principles to them, according to their sources.

Our brains and minds are fantastic. Our minds think very quickly. Experts estimate that the mind thinks between 60,000 – 80,000 thoughts a day. If we break that down, we'll have an average of 2500 – 3,300 thoughts per hour, an average of 40-55 thoughts per minute and about one thought per second. That's incredible!

However, more amazing than this is the speed at which our brain sees images. *Mail Online of 20th January 2014,* states the findings of a team of neuroscientists, who discovered that the human brain can identify a dozen images flashing by in the fraction of a second at record-breaking speed. These U.S. researchers discovered that the human brain can interpret images that the eye sees in just 13 milliseconds. Now, that's fast! Therefore, we must be swift in deciding what to cast down, what to bring into subjection and what to follow. This can be a challenge, but with the Holy Spirit on our side, it is doable.

Test the Spirits

To discern whether an image projected on your mind's eye is from Satan, self, or God, you must first do as the Bible prescribes: *"test the spirits"* according to John 4:1 *"Beloved, do not believe every spirit, but test the spirits to see whether they are from God, for many false prophets have gone out into the world."* as put another way, you must discern the origin of your thoughts or the images you perceive. A flashing image in an empty and idle mind that seems obstructive would be of Satan. An image born in the mind, the painting of a picture, maybe from self while a living flow of pictures coming from the innermost being, when your inner being was quietly focused on Jesus, is of the Lord.

Secondly, you must test the content or ideas according to 1 John 4:5 *"They are of the world: therefore speak they of the world, and the world heareth them."* Satanic thoughts and images are usually negative, destructive, pushy, fearful, and accusative. They violate the nature of God and the Word of God. They are afraid to be tested, are puffed up and are usually accompanied by Ego appeals. Images that originate from self are usually presented as paintings of things that you have learned. They are based on past experiences and acquired knowledge whereas images that come from God are instructive, edifying, comforting and accompanying visions, which are opened to being tested.

Thirdly, you must test the fruits of the picture or your thoughts according to Matthew 7:15-20 *"Beware of false prophets, which come to you in sheep's clothing, but inwardly they are ravening wolves. Ye shall know them by their fruits. Do men gather grapes of thorns, or figs of thistles? Even so every good tree bringeth forth good fruit; but a corrupt tree bringeth forth evil fruit. A good tree cannot bring forth evil fruit; neither can a corrupt tree bring forth good fruit. Every tree that bringeth not forth good fruit is hewn down, and cast into the fire. Wherefore by their fruits ye shall know them."*

Satanic imagery brings with it fear, compulsion, bondage, anxiety, confusion, inflated egos, and the likes. Self-prompted imagery results in variable manifestations include confusion and pride. While Holy Spirit projected images and visions result in quickened faith, power, peace, good fruit, enlightenment, knowledge, humility, direction, and growth among many other good things.

The real battle for men and women who do not know Christ, is the battle in their minds ". . . in whose case the god of this world has blinded the minds of the unbelieving, that they might not see the light of the gospel of the glory of Christ, who is the image of God." (2 Corinthians 4:4 (NAS)

For us, Christian workers, we will on a daily basis have to submit our minds to the Lord because we struggle to see what God wants us to see. Some of these struggles are rooted in deep relational conflict because of satanic opposition. So let us stay in fellowship with the Holy Spirit, who is forever faithful to guide us into all truth.

10. Warfare Realities # 4- Satan Wants to Win

Satan has Great Strength, and his Intention is to Destroy Us and to give no Credence to the Cause of Christ.

Satan is a Real Creature

Apostle Peter counsels us to *"Be sober, be vigilant; because your adversary the devil, as a roaring lion, walketh about, seeking whom he may devour:"* (1 Peter 5:8).

Apostle Paul says *"For we wrestle not against flesh and blood, but against principalities, against powers, against the rulers of the darkness of this world, against spiritual wickedness in high places."* (Ephesians 6:12)

Put together, the information that these men of God have transmitted to us, indicates that Satan is a real creature, spirit in nature and vicious in character. He lives in constant battle mode to destroy Christians and anyone who directly or indirectly promotes the cause of Christ.

Furthermore, he leads a host that is well organized, from the dark side of the spirit realm, to achieve his goals. Therefore, every believer is being sought out for an attack on their lives, and everyone who is not calm, restrained, clear-headed and steady, but who is drunk, inebriated or agitated by Satan's tactics is vulnerable to his deadly advances.

The Bible states that Satan is real, mentioning him several times from Genesis 3:1 to Revelations 12:9. The Bible gives a clear picture of who he is, how he originated, what his goals are, how he was defeated on the cross of Calvary and how he will finally be cast in the lake of fire. This knowledge must be carefully learned and understood by every Christian, especially those believers involved in spiritual warfare so that they will know how to fight the real enemy from the standpoint of victory rather than from a position of defeat.

While He was alive in the flesh, our Lord Jesus met Satan face to face many times in the process of He, the Son of Man, fulfilling His redemptive purpose for mankind. The first of these encounters was in Matthew chapter four after Jesus' baptism and the last was after the Lord arose from the dead. Jesus declared *"I am he that liveth, and was dead; and, behold, I am alive for evermore, Amen; and have the keys of hell and of death,"* *(Revelations 1:18).* In between these, Jesus made 25 references to Satan's existence and plans.

Satan is an angelic being. (Colossians 1:16, Job 1:3) His original name, Lucifer, means great shining light or son of the morning. He was one of the most beautiful creatures and is more intelligent than any human. He was created as a cherub (Ezekiel 28:14) and at that time, was the highest of all beings (Ezekiel 28:14, Jude 9). He was created perfect (Ezekiel 28:12 -13), had a heavenly estate (Jude 6), and was the guardian of God's glory. (Ezekiel 28). Lucifer was special to God.

According to Ezekiel 28, Satan allowed his power and beauty to provide an occasion for his sin. He developed a faulty perception of his self and so his heart became filled with pride (1 Timothy 3:6, Isaiah 14:13) which was the nature of his sin.

However, the real cause of his sin was his faulty perception of God, the world and himself. He chose to personally use his ability to make the decision to rebel against God, with the intent to bring Him into subjection. Today he attacks us in the same arena by providing false imagery in our minds with the intent that we will embrace them and disobey of our own free will and even rebel against God. Satan is indeed a deceiver!

Satan's fall is stretched over several millennia.

He fell first at the point of his negative choice toward the sovereignty of God; this happened in heaven. He developed a faulty perception of himself, so his heart became filled with pride, during which he declared the five *"I will's"* of Isa. 14:12-17 & Ezek. 28:15. He said *"I will ascend into heaven,"* a reference to the throne room of God. Satan wanted to take over God's place. *"I will exalt my throne above the stars of God."* Satan wanted to rule angels. *"I will also sit upon the mount of the congregation in the sides of the north."* Satan wanted to rule independently over the earth. *"I will ascend above the heights of the clouds."* Or, "I will be supreme." He desired to displace God as the sovereign of the universe. *"I will be like the most High."* Satan's power lust; "I will be God." So God cast him out of heaven and down to earth.

However, he who is *"... the prince of the power of the air ... now worketh in the children of disobedience"* (Eph.2:2)

Even the powerful Michael, the archangel, found Satan to be a challenge. (Dan. 10:3) Even though he is fallen, he is powerful and still has restricted access to the heavenly realms from which he and his cohorts were cast out. Job 1:6 records *"Now there was a day when the sons of God came to present themselves before the LORD, and Satan came also among them."* Again, we see Satan standing as a lying spirit in the presence of God in 2 Chr. 18:18-21: *"And Micaiah said, "Therefore hear the word of the LORD: I saw the LORD sitting on his throne, and all the host of heaven standing on his right hand and on his left. And the LORD said, 'Who will entice Ahab the king of Israel, that he may go up and fall at Ramoth-Gilead?' And one said one thing, and another said another. Then a spirit came forward and stood before the LORD, saying, 'I will entice him.' And the LORD said to him, 'By what means?' And he said, 'I will go out, and will be ¹a lying spirit in the mouth of all his prophets.' And he said, 'You are to entice him, and you shall succeed; go out and do so.'*

The second phase of Satan's fall will happen in the middle of the tribulation when he will be denied access to heaven. *"The great dragon was hurled down—that ancient serpent called the devil, or Satan, who leads the whole world astray. He was hurled to the earth, and his angels with him." (Rev. 12:9)* According to Biblical last days' timeline, Satan's permanent banishment from heaven will occur in the latter part of the seven-year tribulation. It is possible that the raptured Christians, you and me, will witness this eviction battle. Because Satan spends most of his time accusing saints before God, it will be a joyous relief to have such an evil creature removed from heaven. However, he will not appreciate this; he will go into a fit of rage and focus all his energy on causing as much death and destruction on earth as possible; hence the Great Tribulation. At this point, Satan will know that the countdown to his final destruction has begun, that his time is short, and that will fuel his wrath.

The last phase of Satan's fall is at the end of the millennial reign of Christ when he will be cast into the lake of fire. *"And the devil that deceived them was cast into the lake of fire and brimstone, where the beast and the false prophet are and shall be tormented day and night forever and ever."(Rev. 20:10).* This will be Satan's final fall. *"Thou hast defiled thy sanctuaries by the multitude of thine iniquities, by the iniquity of thy traffick; therefore, will I bring forth a fire from the midst of thee, it shall devour thee, and I will bring thee to ashes upon the earth in the sight of all them that behold thee.* (Ezek. 28:18).

So where we are in terms of Satan's fall and who are we dealing with? We are in the first phase of Satan's fall. We are dealing with the fallen but yet powerful, vindictive, lying, deceptive creature who has no way of fulfilling his original purpose and spends a lot of time going back and forth to heaven to accuse the brethren. His purpose is to deceive us into believing lies with the intent to have us discredit the Lord, and in the process completely destroy our lives. He fell because pride was found in his heart, which was encouraged by faulty thinking and imagery about his status in relation to God and the world. He has been using the same strategy to cause the destruction of man. As spiritual people, we must be aware of his plans and be able to counteract them. This brings us to our next point.

11. Understanding Strongholds

In an army, generals and colonels plan and strategize, but lower ranks execute tasks. Similarly, in Satan's Force, Satan assigns tasks to a "strong man" which can be a principality, a power or a ruler of darkness, for example, who will second lesser demons under his command to help in the work (Mt. 25-29; Dan. 10:2-6, 12-14). These lesser demons are named by what they do, for example, "Fear," "Anger," "Lust," "Pride," "Deception," etc.

Satan also assigns powerful demons as generals, captains or leaders to oversee the work against various communities, people groups and nations as well. Persia was controlled by demons that were organized under the command of a very powerful demon, who took the role as the *"Prince of Persia."* Demons organized in this way set up strongholds from where they execute their diabolical tasks.

In ancient communities, strongholds were points, which were hard to defeat, because of their design; walls, locations, which were on hilltops or islands, along with the offensive capabilities of an army within. The army could launch attacks, and then retreat to the safety of walled cities. Thus, each point of operation became a *"stronghold."*

In Guyana, we have an example of a stronghold as depicted by the structure on Fort Island. Fort Zeelandia was set up on this island in the 18th century at the mouth of the Essequibo River. The Fort was a square building, equipped with guns and four ramparts, inside of which were three covered redoubts, having flat roofs with embrasures, serving for barracks for soldiers and a powder magazine.[40] The relics of the fort with the cannons are still present after three centuries. I visited it a few weeks ago.

This picture of the physical stronghold is used to explain the spiritual stronghold. Spiritual strongholds are represented in scripture; in the same way, physical strongholds are represented. They are points of operation, where attacks are waged on outlying areas. They become points of offensive operations, which are hard to remove unless a concentrated effort is made to remove them. [41] The best way to deal with strongholds is to prevent their construction in the first place, by being on guard against the enemy individually, like the church, and also by restricting ungodly legislations through the governments of our nations.

In history, strongholds played a vital role; no army could successfully defeat an opponent and let their stronghold stand within conquered territory. One of the main objectives of armies was to remove strongholds within conquered territory. We as the Lord's army need to take notice of demonic objectives, and remove strongholds. Like conquerors of old, we need to target the spiritual strongholds of our enemy; Satan.[42]

A great Old Testament example of this is seen in the Book of Joshua chapters five and six, when the Lord miraculously destroyed the walls of the city of Jericho by the shout of His people, to establish a grand takeover of the entire region.

"The fortifications of Jericho were massive... The walls were structured on a three-tiered plan. The walls started with an earthen rampart, or embankment, which ran from ground level upwards on an incline to a stone retaining wall - the second tier. The stone

---

[40] http://military.wikia.com/wiki/Fort_Zeelandia_(Guyana)
[41] http://www.truthnet.org/Spiritual-warfare/8Spiritual-Strongholds/Strongholds-spiritual.htm
[42] Ibid

retaining wall stood 12 to 15 feet in height (4-5m) on top of the earthen embankment. On top of the stone retaining wall stood another wall made of mud-bricks, 6 feet (2m) thick, and 20 to 26 feet (6-8m) high. Together these two walls combined to form a fortification, 32 to 41 feet high."[43]

"At their base, the walls of Jericho stood 46 feet (14m) above ground level outside the retaining wall. To the Israelites below, Jericho seemed impenetrable. The illusion created by the two walls on the bottom, and the large wall at the crest of the embankment, seemed to stand nearly 10 stories in height from ground level! From this height, the Israelites must have seemed like ants, and surely were deemed no threat whatsoever."[44] However, the greater force of Yahweh destroyed the stronghold!

A later example of this is seen in the construction and the conquering of Constantinople. Constantine created Constantinople (Byzantium) as the capital city of the Eastern Roman Empire in 330. Constantinople was a stronghold; the seat of Byzantine Christianity for more than 1100 years.[45] However, Mehmet II demonstrated his supremacy in 1453, when he hired the famous Hungarian gunsmith Urban to construct cannons of sizes unheard of before. With these cannons, he was able to pound the walls, which affected the fall of Constantinople. Again, the stronger force prevailed!

Like natural strongholds, Satan sets up spiritual strongholds in societies. A stronghold is a point of operation from which Satan can keep the unbeliever captive or the believer incapacitated. The Apostle Paul said: *"For though we walk in the flesh, we do not war according to the flesh. For the weapons of our warfare are not carnal but mighty in God for pulling down strongholds, casting down*

---

[43] http://www.israel-a-history-of.com/walls-of-jericho.html
[44] Ibid
[45] https://www.thoughtco.com/constantinople-capital-of-eastern-roman-empire-119706

arguments and every high thing that exalts itself against the knowledge of God, bringing every thought into captivity to the obedience of Christ," (2 Cor. 10:3-5)

In most countries, people groups and major movements, there are structures of demons assigned to defeat and control the people who are associated with belief systems that are false or that oppose God. These structures of demons also affect churches, Christian ministries, families, and individuals as well. No one gets overlooked; those doing the Lord's work receive special attention from Satan and the kingdom of darkness, while those who are deceived by the lies and strategies are constantly harassed! Gaining insights of these things is important for us to know and understand who we are fighting against; a Strongman. This helps us to know when and how to pray for God's power and protection strategically.

Various Types of Strongholds

Spiritual strongholds are demonic fortresses of thoughts that hide the intentions of evil spirits which control, dictate, and influence the attitudes and behavior of individuals or masses, with the intent to bring oppression and discouragement, thus filtering and coloring how individuals or groups view or react to ideas, situations, circumstances, or people.

There are various types of strongholds:

1.   *Personal strongholds* operate from the level of the mind and find strength in a collection of ideas that are in agreement with Satan's plan for people's lives. Usually, these ideas are opposed to God's truth and bring individuals under the subjugation of the devil's lies.

The physiology of personal strongholds is as follows: As individuals entertain thoughts and participate in activities that are contrary to the will of God, they open up themselves to demonic inhabitation in the areas of their lives they performed such actions. When these thoughts and activities become habitual, they allow spiritual fortifications to be built around those demonic spirits and their influences. Eventually, the individuals become accustomed to responding to the influence and control of the spirits, so much so that they believe that the suggestions of the spirits are the voices of their own minds. After the deception takes place, demons continue to set up circumstances to facilitate temptations and monitor the individual's response.

However, if the affected individual is a Christian, demons continue their sinister construction of strongholds, by arousing the individual's thoughts and emotions until they are too confused to remember to pray or read Scriptures. They cause persons to misperceive situations in order to damage their relationships with others and the Lord. Through demonic agitation, persons develop wrong conclusions about other people's actions toward them, causing further problems.

The best way to deal with personal strongholds is not to allow them in the first place. Pastor Rick Warren said: "When you give the devil a foothold into your life, he takes a stronghold... If you give Satan control of one little part of your life, he will soon take over the whole thing. You give him a foothold into your life, and he turns it into a stronghold."[46]

Personal strongholds may operate through physical objects associated with ungodly soul ties from past relationships; objects used in witchcraft or psychic activities, objects used for demonic games, or artifacts that are associated with ungodly worship practices.

---

[46] http://pastorrick.com/devotional/english/principles-for-personal-change-strongholds

Satan can also use books, music, movies, and software as a means of personal strongholds. Books related to astrology and horoscopes, books related to Satanism, witchcraft and New Age, pornographic materials, hard rock music and videos, movies with occultic messages, extreme violence, excessive obscene language, or explicit sexual contents and violent computer games software can be problematic.

2.   *Ancestral strongholds* operate through general sins and iniquities that are associated with bloodlines. Idolatry is one of the methods used to build ancestral strongholds. Speaking of idolatry in families, God gave a serious warning in the Ten Commandments. He said; *"Thou shalt not bow down thyself to them, nor serve them: for I the Lord thy God am a jealous God, visiting the iniquity of the fathers upon the children unto the third and fourth generation of them that hate me." (Ex. 20:5)*

Ancestral or generational strongholds form, because of sins perpetuated in a family in a number of generations. Generational strongholds are similar to original sin curses because they can be passed down on a generational basis. They differ, however, in that generational strongholds do not impose eternal judgment. They bring judgment or bondage during an individual's life, reducing the quality of life, until that individual addresses the issues and destroys the stronghold(s).

Moses told the new generation of Israelites, who were born in the Wilderness, and who were preparing to enter the Promised Land that they would not enter unless they deal with their own personal sins, and the sins of their fathers. *"Those of you who are left will waste away in the lands of their enemies because of their sins; also because of their fathers' sin, they will waste away. But if they will confess their sins and the sins of their fathers - their treachery against me and their hostility toward me, which made me hostile toward them so that I sent them into the land of their enemies - then when their uncircumcised hearts are humbled, and they pay for their sin, I will remember my covenant with Jacob and my covenant with Isaac and my covenant with Abraham, and I will remember the land." (Lev. 26:39-42)*

Ancestral strongholds may show up as some kind of illness. For example, in some families, it may be cancer, in others, chronic diseases, and yet in others, it may be some kind of mental illness. These problems pass from generation to generation, and even though salvation breaks the severity of the effects of these strongholds, still, good health practices, deliverance, and spiritual warfare may be necessary to protect the believer from demonic assault. In addition, believing families need to learn how to stand in the victory that Christ bought on the cross!

Furthermore, if demons have entered into a family through curses, handed down bloodlines through hexes, spells, curses or pacts before people became Christians, those things should be acknowledged and broken because demons usually don't leave on their own accord, and when they don't, the remedy to get rid of them is casting them out in the name of Jesus.

An example of the effects of a generational stronghold is seen in the Book of St. Mark, where Jesus deals with the situation of an ailing child. Jesus didn't have the boy confess the sins or iniquities of his ancestors, but He immediately cast out the demons that entered into the child through the curse. The curse was probably already broken, and all that was left to do was just to cast the demons out, (Mk. 9:17-27). In a similar way, we can deal with ancestral strongholds, where demons affect persons lives before they became Christians. Even though the curses are broken when they become Christians, the demons must be dealt with.

3.   *Communal strongholds* affect communities and cultures in society, through a collection of regulations, acts, and laws, established in the social and legal framework within a specific

region, that are in agreement with Satan's intentions, and are against God's righteous plan for the people.

There are some root sins described in the Bible, which defile both individuals and the related community where they are allowed to perpetuate. These sins will separate us from God's presence, protection, and blessings, and they defile communities as well.

The Bible indicates that communities and places can be blessed or cursed based on the actions of the people who live there.

In Gen. 4:10-11 God asked Cain "What hast thou done? The voice of thy brother's blood crieth unto me from the ground. And now art thou cursed from the earth, which hath opened her mouth to receive thy brother's blood from thy hand."

 Leviticus 18:25 states, "the land is defiled: therefore I do visit the iniquity thereof upon it, and the land itself vomiteth out her inhabitants."

Also, Ezra 9:11 states, "The land, unto which ye go to possess it, is an unclean land with the filthiness of the people ... which have filled it from one end to another with their uncleanness."

Communal strongholds are established through land defilement, through the sins of the people, through the worship of other gods and idols, and through occult practices in people groups or communities. Just as carcasses attract the vultures of the air, communal sins and defilement of land attracts spiritual wickedness. When the land has been defiled, demons cluster and form communal strongholds which advance to take control of those communities.

Territorial spirits have no authority to move into an area without permission, but certain conditions which we have mentioned above, give them the authority to set up a base from which they rule over the people in that area. When a community has been inhabited by persons who promote ungodly practices, the land becomes contaminated or defiled, and these spirits gain legal, spiritual right to remain there and keep the inhabitants captive.

In some cases, the spirits seem to be so fixed on a particular house, stream, or geographic location, and everyone living in the immediate area is affected by physical sickness, mental illness, or serious demonic attacks. There is a general belief in Guyana that certain kinds of "dutch spirits" are associated with the tamarind trees, and the silk cotton trees planted around cemeteries. There have also been several episodes of demon possession at Kimbia; which was a prominent National Service site up in the Berbice River, and on Fort Island; where the remains of an Old Dutch fort stands.

Generally, to deal with communal strongholds, we must first understand what allowed them in, and what permits them to keep being active. They are perpetuated as the traditions, the beliefs, the same evil sins, attitudes, and cultures of the past generations continue in the present generation. Just as with people, demons remain as generational curses in communities until they are ejected by the blood of Jesus through spiritual warfare.

4.   *Terrestrial strongholds* control activities over larger territories or nations. Territorial spirits energize an entire geographic area with influences of the demonic hierarchy. (Eph. 6:12) The book of Daniel gives us a glimpse into the nature of this level of demonic activity: *"Fear not, Daniel: for from the first day that thou didst set thine heart to understand, and to chasten thyself before thy God, thy words were heard, and I am come for thy words. But the prince of the kingdom of Persia withstood me one and twenty days: but, lo, Michael, one of the chief princes, came to help me..."* *(Dan. 10:10-12).*

In Guyana, there are several communal and national strongholds that can be readily identified. For example, our constitution and legal system allow for obeaism (legalized in the 1970s), abortion (legalized in 1995) and gambling (legalized in 2007). From 1998 the law in Guyana also gives the same privileges to reputed partners, who have lived together for more than 5 years as married couples. This indirectly quietly equates adultery with marriage. Now, there is also a widespread erection of large religious idols across the nation under the idea of freedom of religion. However, these are communal strongholds. Further, presently there is a bill waiting to be tabled from the LGBT advocates, which proposes marriage of gays locally - the Bible calls this *"an abomination."(Lev. 20:13)*

The Bible shows that there is a connection between God, people, land, and geography, based on the people's attitude and relationship to God at any given time. For example, the motive of the builders of the tower of Babel was to make a name for themselves, and to also prevent the people from being scattered across the earth, (Gen 11:8-9). They built the monument for themselves to call attention to their abilities and achievements, instead of giving glory to God. When God observed what a powerful force/ territorial stronghold their unity of purpose created, He confused their language, causing them to speak many different languages so they would not understand each other. By doing this, God thwarted their plans. He also scattered the people of the city all over the face of the earth. Depending on people's attitudes in nations, God *"increaseth the nations, and destroyeth them: he enlargeth the nations, and straiteneth them again,"* (Job 12:23). Sometimes, through our willful refusal to honor the Lord nationally, He removes His protection from a nation, and Satan finds fertile grounds to carry out his plans.

So, Satan has demons; fallen angels, principalities, powers, and rulers of the darkness (Eph. 6, Col. 1), assigned to each of the levels in his army, with each level more powerful than the ones below it. Thus, there are strongholds over nations, regions, cities, neighborhoods, and places of idol worship, places of work, churches, homes, and individuals.

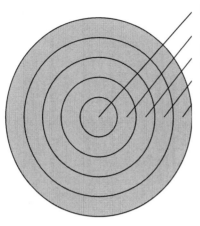

Personal stronghold
Ancestoral stronghold
Communal stronghold
Terrestrial stronghold
Celestial stronghold

As we move outwards, each level of stronghold have larger influence and is more powerful.

Types of Strongholds

5.   *Celestial strongholds* are like territorial strongholds that operate on a higher and larger scale. They may control several countries in a specific geographic area, like in the case of the ISIS spirits that operate in the Middle East. They usually involve cosmic warfare that affects both space and the earth.

As we reflect again on Daniel chapter 10, we would also see the importance of prayer in dealing with strongholds that grip society. God answers prayers, even if it takes a while. Perseverance is the key, God always comes through. It has been correctly said that prayer is not preliminary to the battle, prayer is the battle. So to overcome the strongman, we must engage in spiritual warfare, and persevere! The warfare we experience is just a small fraction of what is taking place in the heavenlies. We are not alone in our battles. Our Lord Jesus, Michael, Gabriel and all of God's heavenly hosts are backing us as we engage in the act of spiritual warfare.

God's people are under attack all of the time, and angels and demons are constantly in conflict in the unseen world because of us. If it seems to you that you are alone, or something must be wrong, because you face these things more than others, remember that all who seek to serve and advance God's kingdom are attacked.

Strongholds hinder Progress and promote Destruction

The Apostle Paul was conscious of this when he wrote to the Thessalonians saying *"Wherefore we would have come unto you, even I Paul, once and again; but Satan hindered us."(1 Thessalonians 2:18)* Satan works at preventing progress from coming to nations; whether it be gospel work or essential services.

UNICEF reported that more than 30 million children are unimmunized either because vaccines are unavailable, because health services are poorly provided or inaccessible, or because families are uninformed or misinformed about when and why to bring their children for immunization. [47]

Statista, reported that the number of global deaths due to lack of vaccination in 2002, by disease is as follows: Pneumococcal is 1,612,000, Measles is 610,000, Hepatitis B is 557,000, Rotavirus is 449,000, Haemophilus Influenzae B is 386,000, Pertussis is 294,000 Tetanus is 213,000, Yellow fever is 30,000, Meningococcal is 26,000, Japanese encephalitis is 14,000 Diphtheria is 5,000 and Polio is 1,000. This situation was due to lack of vaccination. What about the lack of water and food? What about the lack of medicine for diarrheal disease, and respiratory tract infection? [48]

On the other hand, the devil is very aggressive in providing services that will enhance his plan to *"to steal and kill and destroy" (John 10:10).*

Take abortion services, for example, *Guttmacher Institute* reported that during 2010–2014, an estimated 56 million induced abortions occurred each year worldwide. This number represents an increase from 50 million annually during 1990–1994. The global annual rate

---

[47] https://www.unicef.org/immunization/index_why.html
[48] https://www.statista.com/statistics/265002/deaths-due-to-lack-of-vaccination-in-2002/

of abortion was estimated at 35 abortions per 1,000 women of childbearing age (i.e., those 15–44 years old) in 2010–2014. Globally, 25% of pregnancies ended in abortion in 2010–2014.[49]

The above-mentioned examples are just a few of the ways Satan attacks individuals, churches, and nations. If our foundations are strong, he will not be able to penetrate us easily. But if there is an erosion in our foundations, he will intrude and attack the structures and the institutions of our lives, churches and nations, using those vices that come with *"the lust of the flesh, and the lust of the eyes, and the pride of life" (1John 2:16)*, as basis to attack all of the strong values that are so deeply rooted in our Godly traditions.

Satan functions as the father of lies, and he is a murderer according to John 8:44. Death and lies seem to go hand in hand. As we review Satan's strategies over the centuries of his assault on God's plan for individuals, the church and the world, we see his success was generally based on lies.

Satan's success has been significant across the globe. The main structure he has been using to leverage his success in academia. He understands the pride that smart people feel. He attacks them when they think they are smarter than everybody else, and could come up with something new and different. He lures them in the pursuit of lies under the guise of "new truths," and he gets them, through secular humanism, for example, to deny the existence of absolute truth.

I learned that many colleges in the United States, including Harvard, Yale, and Princeton, which started over 300 years ago were once Bible-based schools on rich Christian histories. However, they all fell first in the area of science, from embracing the Christian worldview of creation to naturalistic philosophy which opposes the Genesis

---

[49] https://www.guttmacher.org/fact-sheet/induced-abortion-worldwide

account of human origin. "Once Christians began adopting a naturalistic view, including evolution or earth history over millions of years, it didn't take long for the rest of their faith to come crumbling down. They had given up the Bible as their starting point and had accepted naturalistic science instead."[50]

The Psalmist David asked the question *"When the foundation is destroyed, what can the righteous do?" (Psalm 11:3)* Cracks in the foundation of academia in society have led to a collapse of the Christian worldview across the world.

Identifying Strongholds

All spiritual strongholds have their origin in the realm of the spirit but affect people and the natural world at various levels. As we move from personal strongholds to celestial strongholds, they increase in strength and in the geographic and cosmic areas as described earlier.

Some demons seem to have much more flexibility; they roam the earth, while other spirits, such as ancestral or guardian spirits have geographical restrictions to their power and capabilities. (Mark 5:10)

As mentioned earlier, in some cases, the spirit seems to be so fixed in a particular house, stream, or geographic location, that everyone living in the immediate area is affected by sickness, mental illness, or serious attack.

However, they may also be viewed in relation to whether they are known or unknown, and as to the severity of their effects, that is,

---

[50] Bodie Hodge, Harvard, Yale, Princeton, Oxford — Once Christian? June 27, 2007 https://answersingenesis.org/christianity/harvard-yale-princeton-oxford-once-christian/

whether they cause minor, moderate or severe assaults on lives and properties.

Identifying strongholds is of critical importance if we will successfully expel them at any level. Paul tells us that the kingdom of darkness has a high Arche. By combining Ephesians 6:12 and Colossians 1:16, we know of principalities, authorities, powers, dominions, thrones, rulers of darkness and spirits of wickedness.

Also, throughout the Bible, many idols and false gods were named. So we know of Baal (Num 22:41), Dagon (Judges 16:23), Baalim and Ashtaroth (Judges 2:11-13), Ashtoreth and Milcom (I Kings 11:5), Chemosh and Milcom (I Kings 11:33), Succoth (2 Kings 17:30), Benoth (2 Kings 17:30), Adrammelech (2 Kings 17:31), Molech (2 Kings 23:10), Prince of Persia (Daniel 10), Prince of Greece (Daniel 10:20), Queen of Heaven (Jer 44:17-25), Merodach (Jer 50:2), Moloch and Remphan (Acts 7:43), Diana of Ephesus (Acts 19:27), Wormwood (Rev 8:11), Abaddon (Rev 9:11) and Apollyon (Rev 9:11). They also had specific areas of influence.

It would be noteworthy to observe that demons don't die; however, in our world today we do not hear of these names mentioned in the Bible. So are these demonic entities still present or not? I believe they are; in some cases using the same names but generally operating under other names, and doing the same harm.

In the New Testament accounts of our Lord's encounter with demoniacs, He identified the spirit by its function, He had little or no conversation with them, and He commanded them to leave by the power of the Spirit.

In one case, the disciples were unable to deliver a child from an evil spirit. Jesus delivered the child and taught the disciples that the higher the rank of the evil spirit, the more spiritual power is needed to bind it. Fasting and prayers supplies that power. He said, *"Howbeit this kind goeth not out but by prayer and fasting."(*Mt.

17:21)

Strongholds can manifest at Different Levels

Many Strongholds affect peoples' lives in various ways:

At the *lowest level,* strongholds may affect people in minor ways so that their impact on lives is insignificant. However, if recognized, they should be dealt with so that they are not allowed to fester and eventually get to another level.

At the *moderate level,* strongholds may affect people to the extent that they can still effectively fulfill their daily duties, but are plagued with issues and challenges on a regular basis.

But, at the *extreme level,* demonic strongholds greatly hinder any one or combination of areas in people's lives: spiritually, socially, materially, or physically.

Strongholds that hinder people's spiritual lives include greed, materialism, worldliness, unforgiveness, bitterness, and sexual sins. Strongholds that hinder people's social lives include sexual sins, unforgiveness, bitterness, temper tantrums, materialism, alcohol addiction and discrimination (gender, racial, ethnic, etc.). Strongholds that hinder people's material lives include greed, selfishness, and compulsive gambling. While, strongholds that hinder people's physical lives include alcohol addiction, unhealthy eating habits and addiction to unhealthy foods.

Once the stronghold is identified, plans should be put in place to deal with it. In dealing with strongholds, it is prudent to prayerfully search for not only the severity of strongholds but also which area(s) of one's life they affect, since they may be affecting a combination of areas. Some persons with strongholds may also have wounded spirits to be dealt with.

12. Warfare Realities # 5- Don't Be Afraid of the Enemy

*We must respect Our Arch Enemy and
be aware of His Strategies, but
We should not be afraid of Him nor be overly occupied with His
Doings.*

Chained to a soldier in the Roman prison, but yet free in his spirit, in warfare mode, Apostle Paul commands us to *"Put on the whole armor of God that ye may be able to stand against the wiles of the devil." (Eph.6:11)* He considers every Christian as having a war to fight against Satan and his numerous, sturdy, and subtle cohorts; and that therefore we would need much strength, much courage, to put on the whole armor of God, and garner the skills to use it.

"Put on the whole armor of God" refers to the fact that life itself is a battlefield, not a playground, nor a place of comfort and ease, but of hard conflict, with foes within and without. *"Put on the whole armor of God"* is for our protection and aggression too; it is for both offensive and defensive warfare.

Unlike the armor of Saul on David which was made especially for Saul, and was unsuitable for David, the *"armor of God"* is good and well-adapted for use by any and every child of God. God thought of you and created His armor for you. It fits all ages and genders, it can be adapted to all sizes and personality types, and it can *"quench all the fiery darts of the wicked."*(Eph. 6:16) So *"Put on the whole armor of God,"* for each part of your spirit, soul, and body, needs to be protected, and you need suitable weapons to resist and defeat all your foes and to *"be able to stand against the wiles of the devil."*

Though it does not happen frequently, Satan and his cohorts may engage us in open warfare! He operates as an ambusher; he and his demons wait in concealed positions to launch a sudden, surprise attack. Satan deals in wiles and stratagems, which need to be known, watched against and prepared for, with peculiar care by putting *"on the whole armor of God."* Deliverance ministers must understand that not arming oneself is tantamount to ignorance or presumptuousness. Trying to engage in spiritual warfare without the armor is like skydiving without a suit. Obvious destruction is inevitable.

One of the valuable lessons we learn in developing a warfare mentality is to respect the enemy. Satan has been around for eons. He is a powerful creature. His intelligence, skills, and strategies are way beyond what any of us will naturally reach in this life. He is deceptive, cunning and smart and he must be respected for these characteristics. He can transform himself as he sees fit. Even people who are possessed by demons may transform themselves to accomplish evil ends.

In Guyanese folklore, we hear of Ol'Hige, Sukyanti, Kaniama, Bakoo, Massacurra Man and Moongazer. For most of these, the characteristic feature is demonic possession of a human who gets involved in shapeshifting and possessing super-human strength. Our detection of the devil and his cohorts must be by the Holy Spirit working in us. Spiritual perception will enable us to identify spirits, and bring us safety and success.

Satan is a schemer and a very skilled one too. He is very deceptive. He has no red skin or horns, no trident or pitchfork, and does not breathe fire and brimstone. Fire and brimstone make him shudder because he was condemned to the lake of fire. (Mt. 25:41)

1. Dealing with Personal Attacks

On a personal level, Satan tends to attack us primarily in three areas: physical, intellectual, and moral. So we have to be able to identify when he is attacking and in which area. Then we must resist his attacks biblically, which enables us to find consistent victory in our spiritual warfare against the enemy of our souls.

The enemy looks for opportunities to attack us physically. Satan attempts to afflict the body just as he tries to afflict the soul and spirit. Jesus said, *"He was a murderer from the beginning" (Jn. 8:44).* Doctor Luke tells us of a woman whom Jesus healed. She *"had been crippled by a spirit for 18 years ... whom Satan [had] kept bound for 18 long years." (Luke 13).* Like the numerous physical healings by exorcism seen in the Gospels, this woman was delivered by the casting out of the spirit in her.

Even though sickness exists in the world because of the original sin of Adam and Eve, the Bible reveals various reasons for individuals getting sick. The first, and perhaps most apparent, is Satan caused sicknesses. In regards to physical problems caused by Satan it is essential to remember that as a believer, God is in control of your life. Sometimes illness is a direct physical attack by Satan, but God gets the glory when physical healing occurs through prayer as a counter-strategy, which ensures victory.

When someone is extremely stressed or physically tired, Satan can take advantage of this and launch spiritual attacks on the individual. He also attacks our bodies, when we are exhausted from being too busy or working too hard. He tried it with Elijah, who was tired from his great spiritual success of praying down fire from heaven. Elijah became so discouraged that he wanted to die *(I Kg. 19:4).* He tried it again with our Lord Jesus when He was exhausted from 40 days of fasting *(Mt. 4:2),* but the Lord resisted him. Knowing this, Jesus called His disciples to rest when they were exhausted from their busy ministry *(Mk. 6:31).*

Satan not only causes illnesses, but he attempts to cause premature death. He may accomplish this by tempting people to commit suicide or make people become overwhelmed by the fear of disease or accidents, which could result in death. God protects Christians, and He controls our lives, so Satan cannot touch us physically nor take our lives without the knowledge of God.

Satan cannot take the life of a believer in an intrusive way as is seen in the story of Job, but he can tempt one to take his own life. The Spirit of God may woo one away from such act, but God does not overrule the human will. If Satan tempts, and the person yields to commit suicide, God will not override the action of his will. If as a warfare minister you discern a spirit of death hovering over someone's life, you can bind it in the name of Jesus, and encourage the person to resist the devil and be set free!

In the case of illness, remember that God who made the human body has the power to heal that body. Whenever you sense a physical condition, as an attack from Satan, let wisdom prevail; seek medical attention, but also request prayers of your prayer support group, including those with the spiritual gift of healing. Claim his promises for healing when you experience physical attacks from Satan. *"But He was wounded for our transgressions; He was bruised for our iniquities; the chastisement of our peace was upon Him, and with His stripes, we are healed." (Isa. 53:5)* *"Beloved, I wish above all things that thou mayest prosper and be in health, even as thy soul prospereth." (3 Jn. 1: 2)*

Satan not only attacks people physically but mentally. Jesus said in John 8:44 *"there is no truth in him ... he is a liar..."* He intends to deceive the mind. He did this to Eve and have been doing this ever since. *"You will not surely die" (Gen. 3:4)* he said to her, yet Eve died spiritually, and all her descendants died with her. That one lie affected the entire human race. Discerning the voice of the evil one is of paramount importance in resisting him.

Also, Satan comes against us morally. St. John said *"...the devil has been sinning from the beginning. (1 Jn. 3:8)* He is an experienced sinner, who never ceases to bring temptations against the moral side of mankind. He encourages *"the lust of the flesh, the lust of the eyes, and the pride of life" (1 Jn. 2:16).* But God has put provisions in place, so we can overcome these devilish attacks,

The Apostle John explains that *"...the reason the Son of God appeared was to destroy the devil's work." (1 Jn 3:8)* This is a done deal! Jesus has come and has already destroyed the devil's work when He died on the cross of Calvary. Satan has been defeated! There is no reason to be afraid of him. Eliminating fear from one's life is a significant factor in overcoming the strongman.

If fear remains active in someone's life, it will captivate thoughts, paralyze forward momentum and suffocate one's God-given destiny. But, God has given us the authority to overcome every obstacle Satan attempts to set in our path. *"For God hath not given us the spirit of fear; but of power, and of love, and of a sound mind." (2 Tim. 1:7)* No matter the situation or circumstance, God has given us the power to break the spirit of fear, and the strength to fight victoriously against the tactics of the enemy in every area of our lives.

If allowed, fear will infuse itself in all the critical aspects of our lives. Fear will squeeze the very life out of people's dreams, and plans for the future. It will even act as a stimulus to physical ailments that may shorten one's life span. However, the anointing of Christ rests on believers. *"And it shall come to pass in that day, that his burden shall be taken away from off thy shoulder, and his yoke from off thy neck, and the yoke shall be destroyed because of the anointing," (Isa. 10:27).* As we surrender to the Lord, He keeps us protected under His wings, and the anointing of the Holy Spirit destroys every yoke and lifts every burden that weighs us down. The anointing teaches us that we must learn to step out in faith and trust God to deliver us and heal us by crushing the pain that fear brings. We fear God, not the devil!

Another important proactive measure in dealing with Satan's strategies is *"Do not give the devil a foothold." (Eph. 4:27)* Do not allow him to get his foot in the door of your heart. Job understood this when he said, *"I have made a covenant with my eyes; why then should I look upon a young woman?" (Job 31:1)* Let us be careful not to let any compromising situation to develop. Let us be watchful to see if out for weariness or comfort we are allowing our moral guard to drop.

A Godly walk is a powerful strategy against Satan's efforts towards us. The Psalmist David asked *"How can a young man keep his way pure? By living according to your word." (Ps. 119:9)*Then he answers by saying *"I have hidden your word in my heart that I might not sin against you," (Ps. 119:11)*. The Apostle John declares *"We know that anyone born of God does not continue to sin; the one who was born of God keeps him safe, and the evil one cannot harm him,"(1 Jn 5:18)*. Walking godly means not continuing to sin; this activates the second part of that Scripture *"the evil one cannot harm [you]."* Walking godly means giving *"no place"* to the devil. It is a pure and godly walk with God, which shuts the door to Satan's seductions.

A godly walk is supported by filling oneself with the Word of God, even though Satan will still attack. He went to Jesus in the wilderness and said to Him *"If you are the Son of God, tell these stones to become bread." Jesus answered, "It is written: 'Man does not live on bread alone, but on every word that comes from the mouth of God." (Mt. 4:3-4)* Our Lord said, *"It is written"!* As an example of how we can resist the devil with the Word of God. The apostle Paul calls the Word of God, *"the sword of the Spirit" (Eph. 6:17)*.

If you discern an intrusion from Satan and his cohorts, resist him. Live close to God, be obedient to Him and live a pure life. Although the devil comes to steal, kill, and destroy (John 10:10), Jesus has defeated him already, so we can overcome him in Jesus' name! Apostle James said *"Submit yourselves, then, to God. Resist the devil, and he will flee from you. Come near to God, and he will come near to you. Wash your hands, you sinners, and purify your hearts, you double-minded."(Jam. 4:7-8)*

2. Dealing with Church Related Attacks

Satan is most subtle and most dangerous when he operates from within the church, as an angel of light. Even though our arch enemy attacks the church from the outside, his most effective strategy has been to work through the people and even leaders from within the church itself.

The Apostle Paul warns the church in 2 Corinthians 11:13-15 *"For such are false apostles, deceitful workers, transforming themselves into apostles of Christ. And no wonder! For Satan, himself transforms into an angel of light. Therefore it is no great thing if his ministers also transform themselves into ministers of righteousness, whose end will be according to their works."* The Greek word for *"transform"* used here is *"metamorphoó,"* the root of the English terms *"metamorphosis"* and *"metamorphize,"* (Strong's Greek: 3339). The word "transform" indicates that Satan is able to change his outward appearance, by assuming an appearance that does coincide with his sinful nature, nor is representative of his purpose to destroy. Satan "masquerades" through human vessels with the intent to deceive, even in the church.

Paul refers to the false apostles as Satan's ministers who come into the church masquerading themselves as the ministers of righteousness but are there to do the work of their true master; Satan. They operate with the old thief, *"to steal and kill and destroy."(Jn. 10:10)* We have to be able to identify them and deal with them accordingly.

Sometimes we are looking in the wrong places for the wrong indicators. The most dangerous scheme is an inside job. Being a deceiver, Satan will not usually show up in obvious ways. He uses those who claim to believe the Bible and who seem to show reverence in worship, but who are subtly redefining the terms of reference in the kingdom of God. We must be on constant watch to guard against Satan's ploys to introduce doctrinal deviancy from within our ranks.

We must also be intelligently watchful over the church of Christ. Sometimes, *"men will rise up, speaking perverse things, to draw away the disciples after themselves" (Acts 20:30).* We should be careful of people we elect to be leaders, and the scope we give them. We are doing pro-active, preventative spiritual warfare as we continue to place well trained, honest, godly, Spirit-filled men at the helm of the Church.

Church problems may indicate the presence of demonic influences in numerous areas: These may include church splits, leadership problems or relationship issues within the board and elders. Lack of focused vision or general stagnation problems, backbiting, gossip, or general discontent, which may also indicate a subtle intrusion of the serpent. Frequent music or worship problems, history of constant financial worries, inability to retain Sunday school or youth ministry growth over several years, may also be indicative of demonic advantage. Leadership difficulties, marriage splits, history of leadership indiscretions, difficulty in maintaining spiritual growth, little or no success at community outreach and evangelism over the years, are symptoms. Furthermore, historical difficulty to have involvement with other churches in interchurch events, history of sickness or illness especially within leadership families, and lack of effective conversion growth may be signs as well. Satan needs space and time to establish his schemes, but when we do not give him these, he will be stifled. The scriptures say, *"Submit yourselves therefore to God. Resist the devil, and he will flee from you."(Jam. 4:7)*

Let us prepare ourselves and those under our supervision to know the true doctrines and ways of God, through authentic biblical Christianity. Let us train our minds and eyes to identify truth. Let us cling tenaciously to the Word of God, and utterly reject any teaching and any teacher who is not completely in accord with the doctrines of the Bible. Let us learn how to hear the voice of God, so we can quickly identify the usurper. Only then can we be able to deduce the counterfeit from the real.

Satan not only tries to creep into the church through false disciples (*Mt. 13*), false ministers (*2 Cor. 11:14-15*), false doctrine (*1 Jn. 2:18*), false religions (*1 Cor. 10:19*) and false philosophies *(Col. 2:8),* he also tries through false morals. (*2 Thess.2:7*) His purpose is *"to steal and kill and destroy."(John 10:10)*

We are to protect the morals in the body of Christ, although in doing so we must be considerate. The Apostle Paul counsels us *"Wherefore let him that thinketh he standeth take heed lest he fall."(1 Cor. 10:12)* He agrees to forgive a brother along with the Corinthian church *"in order that no advantage be taken of us by Satan; for we are not ignorant of his schemes." (2 Cor. 2:11)*

To deal effectively with spiritual strongholds against the church effectively, we must first identify them. Spiritual mapping is an effective way of doing this. A completed map enlightens us and gives information from which to pray intelligently against the strongholds, which communal sins gave permission to enter. From this vantage point, we can deal with the spiritual forces and strongholds that hold us back from fulfilling God's purposes in the church.

Once the spiritual forces over the church have been identified, we can move ahead to minister freedom to the corporate church body, through a multi-stage approach which includes the following: personal repentance of past generational curses and sins, current sins and iniquities, idolatry, victimization, occult objects or practices, trauma at an early age, unforgiveness, and forms of personal defilement through various sins and immorality. By doing this, we shut all doors that were opened in our spiritual hedge of protection through curses and sins.

Satan does his best to intrude through the hedge God builds around us. In Job's case, Satan asked, *"Have you not put a hedge around him and his household and everything he has?"(Job 1:6-12)*. In other words, Satan is seeking God's permission to destroy the hedge of protection. However, in cases like unforgiveness, this protection is not restored unless there is reconciliation of broken relationships between brethren. It is important that we do this because our spiritual authority is leveraged in direct proportion to the harmony of relationships among believers in the church.

Personal repentance may be followed by personal deliverance when there is a need for such. This may take time, and should not be rushed. During this process preaching and teaching on deliverance and inner healing can enhance the outcomes.

After this, the church at a special corporate gathering, for example, during a *Spiritual Emphasis Week-End*, should use the information gathered from the spiritual mapping exercise to bind the Strongman. In all cases, the Strongman is a demon, but he may be using a lesser spirit, a human person or a corrupt social structure as his agent of destruction.

This can be followed by congregational repentance. Here corporate sins of the past and present are identified and repented from. Remit the sins of the past generations, even if these people are dead. Stand in the gap and cry out to God so that the sin and the ensuing consequences will be dealt with. Freedom will follow this action for Jesus said, *"Whose soever sins ye remit, they are remitted unto them; and whose soever sins ye retain, they are retained"* (John 20:23).

The Bible records a situation that existed in Israel because of Saul's sins. Even after he died, David had to deal with it. 2 Samuel 21:1- 3 say *"Then there was a famine in the days of David three years, year after year; and David enquired of the LORD. And the LORD answered, it is for Saul, and for his bloody house, because he slew the Gibeonites.... Wherefore David said unto the Gibeonites, What shall I do for you? and wherewith shall I make the atonement, that ye may bless the inheritance of the LORD?"* David had to make it right with the Gibeonites, in order for the blessings of the Lord to flow in Israel. We, likewise, are able to stand in the stead of another person or group, living or dead that is associated with us and pray that their sins be remitted, so that the consequences of their actions will not affect future generations.

Nehemiah *(Neh. 1:6-7)* and Daniel *(Dan. 9:5-7)* showed us that when remitting generational sins, we must confess our personal sins as well as the corporate sins of our people. Those who remit the sins of others must not fail to identify personally with the sins that were or are being committed, even though they might not personally be guilty of them as they are of other sins.

We can then move on to breaking any known vows or covenants which may have existed, and which can hinder growth and progress in the church.

Finally, we can do what I call a *"Jericho walk."* First, the "praisers" leading in praises to the Lord; then the intercessors crying out for the sins. Let there be shouting, clapping of hands, and raising of hands as powerful weapons of spiritual warfare. And, as the group walks around the building or the lot let them shout Daniel 2:23 *"I thank thee, and praise thee, O thou God of my fathers, who hast given me wisdom and might, and hast made known unto me now what we desired of thee: for thou hast now made known unto us the king's matter."* or other scriptures of victory and clap their hands as in *Ezek. 6:11.* Verbally decree all covenants broken, and verbally establish a new covenant with God. If there are those in the group with a prophetic gift, let them prophesy life and blessings to the ground.

3. Dealing with Satan's Attacks on Society

We may identify spiritual strongholds over towns, cities or areas, the same way we identify them over our church or neighborhood, which is by performing spiritual mapping to determine why the spirits have permission to remain in the area. You will be looking for reasons behind the lands defilement.

Jesus said in the last days "You will hear of wars and rumors of wars, but see to it that you are not alarmed. Such things must happen, but the end is still to come. Nation will rise against nation, and kingdom against kingdom. There will be famines and earthquakes in various places. All these are the beginning of birth pains. "Then you will be handed over to be persecuted and put to death, and you will be hated by all nations because of me. At that time many will turn away from the faith and will betray and hate each other, and many false prophets will appear and deceive many people. Because of the increase of wickedness, the love of most will grow cold," (Matthew 24:6-12). This is Satan at work! It is not political war, nor cultural war, this is primarily spiritual war with political and cultural manifestations.

Satan is trying to control the entire earth by directing governments, *(Dan. 10:13).* Many radical Islamic states are yielding to his power to kill in the name of religion, while many non- Islamic countries are passing "death–laws' like abortion, euthanasia, infanticide, etc. Satan also shows up in nations by deceiving men *(2 Cor.4:4)* and destroying lives. *(Heb. 2:14) The Congressional-Executive Commission on China (CECC)* reports "As of 2015, there were reportedly 34 million more men than women and there are an estimated 62 million "missing girls," those aborted due to a cultural preference for sons and exacerbated by decades of enforced birth limitations. The sex ratio imbalance is a significant factor that contributes to human trafficking, for forced marriage and commercial sexual exploitation."[51] However, every one of those babies is in heaven with their Heavenly Father. Satan may have thwarted their earthly purpose, but their eternal purpose is secured in Christ. To effectively deal with this kind of onslaught on human lives, the church must unite for spiritual warfare, targeting ideologies and legislation in nations.

The devil is also causing widespread persecution of the saints, (*Rev. 2:10*). *Open Doors*, an organization which serves persecuted saints in many countries of the world gives the following statistics: each month there are 722 different forms of violence against Christians. These happen in about 60 countries and may include beatings, physical torture, confinement, isolation, rape, severe punishment, imprisonment, slavery, discrimination in education and employment, and even death. During this same period, 214 churches and Christians properties are destroyed, and 322 Christians are killed for their faith. [52]

Persecution occurs because, in some nations, authoritarian governments seek to control all religious thought and expression. Also, in some nations that are predominantly Islamic, Hindu or Communist, there is hostility towards nontraditional and minority religious groups. The hostility comes more from society than from the government per se. In these nations, we must enter spiritual warfare against the territorial and communal spirits that control geographic areas. To learn more about this, we can review Daniel's method given in the book of Daniel chapter ten. We will gain

---

[51] Jeff Sagnip   Oct 6, 2016, New Report Shows 62 Million "Missing" Girls in China Thanks to Sex-Selection Abortions,
http://www.lifenews.com/2016/10/06/new-report-shows-62-million-missing-girls-in-china-thanks-to-sex-selection-abortions/
[52]What is Christian Persecution?
https://www.opendoorsusa.org/christian-persecution/

valuable insight into the battle in the heavenlies from this event in Daniel's life.

Israel was in captivity, and Daniel took note of it since he was young. However, towards the end of his life, he was fasting and praying for wisdom from God. After 21 days without an answer, an angel appeared to him and told him that since the first day he started to pray God sent a messenger to answer his prayer. However, for 3 weeks the prince of Persia ,the demon who was the territorial ruler of Persia fought against this messenger angel to keep him from getting to Daniel. Michael finally came to join in the battle, so the heavenly courier from God was able to defeat the demonic oppression. He was then able to come to Daniel and complete his mission, by giving God's answer to Daniel.

Satan also works by creating border issues between nations. He promotes schisms in and between nations as he does in churches, (2 Cor. 2:10, 11). Guyana is presently at the receiving end of a border dispute that was settled a long time ago. However, our neighbor, Venezuela holds the position that the Arbitral Award of 1899 for Guyana[53] to occupy its present space is null and void. This is unfortunate; it speaks of jealousy, coveteousness, bullyism and total lack of respect for organized structure, all which flows from the father of lies.

The Israeli–Palestinian conflict has been an ongoing struggle between Israelis and Palestinians for more than 60 years now. Despite a long-term peace process and the general reconciliation of Israel with Egypt and Jordan, Israelis and Palestinians have failed to reach a final peace agreement. Many attempts have been made to broker a two-state solution, involving the creation of an

---

[53] Guyana/Venezuela 1899 Arbitral Award, http://guyanachronicle.com/2016/10/09/guyanavenezuela-1899-arbitral-award

independent Palestinian state, alongside the State of Israel (after Israel's establishment in 1948) but the situation remains unresolved.[54]

National border issues are tricky to pray for because there are Christians living in both countries who may be praying about the matter. Therefore we must bless and not curse the nation that is perceived as the problematic one but at the same time bind the strongholds that manifest themselves; taking into consideration that there may be manifested strongholds in the country you support.

There are people with good intentions all across the world who would like to use their skills, talents, gifting, and resources to make this world a better place but Satan works in nations to prevent essential or needed services; gospel related and otherwise.

From Daniel chapter 10 we understand that there is organization among Satan's forces. He arranges his demons in the same manner God has organized His angels, that is, in a military-like structure. In an army, there are generals, colonels, majors, lieutenants, sergeants, corporals, privates, etc. In Satan's Force, there are principalities, powers, rulers of darkness and spiritual wickedness in high places. (Eph. 6:12). He organizes and uses them to meet out his assault on the world. However, we have the Captain of the Lord's host on our side, and He does not fail in battle.

Once we have set our individual church and its members free, and have participated in a congregational redemption through repentance and confession, binding the Strongman and making open declarations of victory, we can now begin to bring freedom to our neighborhoods, towns, regions, and countries. Special attention must be given to places where demonic activities are usually

---

[54] Israeli–Palestinian conflict
https://en.wikipedia.org/wiki/Israeli%E2%80%93Palestinian_ conflict

prevalent, like mountains or high places, rivers, kokas, streams, fountains, seas, swamps and forests. However, we must be cognizant of the fact that we will be dealing with more powerful spiritual forces as we try to free larger areas. Therefore, we must not exceed our spiritual authority but join with other churches and even larger fellowships to have a greater number of prayer warriors, in unity and cooperation to affect the warfare and effect the anticipated victory.

Also, know that setting a neighborhood, town or city free is only part of the process of redemption. It brings the land from negative to zero. Praise, worship, and other positive spiritual activities are needed to move the land from zero to the positive.[55]

[55] Healing of the Spirit Booklet, http://healingofthespirit.org/our-ministry/healing-of-the-spirit-booklet/ Territorial Spirits PDF

13. Warfare Realities # 6- We Fight from Victory to Victory!

As Believers in Christ, we engage in the act of warfare on the basis of Finished Work of Christ on the Cross.

It must be understood that all the efforts described in earlier chapters must be from the standpoint of victory which is already ours because in Christ we are victorious! Nevertheless, we engage in spiritual warfare to enact that victory in the spheres of our involvement. Therefore, our work is for enforcement rather than for gaining victory.

Jesus won the victory on the cross of Calvary. The Apostle Paul said: "And having spoiled principalities and powers, he made a show of them openly, triumphing over them in it," (Col 2:15).

Can you imagine how demons hung on the body of Jesus, by legions, while He was on the cross trying to make His sufferings more unbearable than they were? Can you see them tormenting His mind to confuse Him so as to thwart His purpose? Can you imagine them screeching in His ears at frequencies that are deafening to humans, to distract Him from His true goal? Yes! They tried their best with all their authority and diabolical powers to overcome the Savior of mankind, but after bearing the legal sufferings of the cross, our Lord stripped off all principalities and powers, took away their rules and authorities, and made a display of them openly.

Yes, as man He suffered at their wicked hands and yes, He died with a broken heart for the sins of the world. As man, He suffered and died, paying the price for sin. But, as God, He permitted and tolerated their antics until He died to save the world. Then, He began to legally use His authority as the Son of God to strip them of their power and authority; He disengaged them, neutralized them, dislodged them, and disarmed them! And then, made a display openly of them!

The pains, sufferings, and shame the Lord Jesus endured on the cross for the sins of the world were the precursors for the victory won. He suffered and died so that the world can be saved. When He was buried and went down to Hades, Christ proclaimed His victory to the spirits imprisoned there.

While this was happening in the realm of the spirit, there were some physical and natural phenomena occurring:

Matthew, Mark, and Luke all reported that on the day Jesus was crucified, the sky turned very dark at the sixth hour of the day. *"Now from the sixth hour there was darkness over all the land unto the ninth hour." (Mt. 27:45)* The word *"darkness"* is the Greek word *skotos*, which refers to something very dark.[56] This sudden and unexplainable darkness covered all the *"land,"* which according to the Greek word *ge*, indicates that the entire earth[57] was dark, not just the small geographical region where Golgotha was located. This tells us that the effects of the cross were for the whole earth!

At that same instant, miles away from Golgotha inside the temple at Jerusalem, an unfathomable, perplexing supernatural event occurred. The massive fortified veil, sixty feet high, thirty feet wide, and an entire handbreadth in thickness, so heavy that it took three hundred priests to handle it, which stood before the Holy of Holies was suddenly split in half from top to bottom! (Mt. 27:51) This happened about the same time when two high priests were about to make their sacrifice. High priest Caiaphas was standing at his

---

[56] Strong's Concordance, 4655. Skotos, σκότος
[57] Strong's Concordance, 1093. Gé, γῆ, γῆς, ἡ

station in the inner court of the temple, getting ready to offer the blood of a spotless Passover lamb. At the exact moment, High Priest Jesus was taking His last breath on the Cross of Calvary, and He exclaimed, "It is finished!"(John 19:30) Matthew and Mark qualified what happened by saying that just before Jesus breathed his last, he *"cried out again in a loud voice" (Mt. 27:50, Mk 15:37)*. It wasn't the cry of a defeated person, but the shout of a victor announcing his victory loudly and broadly: *"It is finished!"* In other words, "The victory is won!" So, when we war, we war from the standpoint of victory!

As the veil was suddenly split in half from top to bottom, Caiaphas, the high priest heard the ripping sounds coming from above and then watched in utter amazement as the veil was torn in half. But, he may have worked it out in his mind, there was no need for a high priest any longer, for the separation between God and man has been obliterate, torn apart, and removed! This was Jesus' doings, His sacrifice opened a new and living way for man to come to his Heavenly Father! Wow!

So while Caiaphas is seeing a destroyed veil, other things are rattling, falling or being displaced around him. For example, on the table of showbread, (Ex 25:23-30) there were four vessels of pure gold usually kept in an orderly fashion, with dishes which served as bread plates, containing 12 breads packed neatly, bowls containing the frankincense, pans or spoons used to sprinkle frankincense, and pitchers for liquid offerings. Suddenly this table was in disarray! Why? Well, there was an earthquake! Matthew 27:51 says, *"...the earth did quake, and the rocks rent."*

The word *"quake"* is the Greek word *seiso*[58], which means to shake, to agitate, or to create a commotion. Basically, the foundations of the earth were responding to the suffering of its creator. A great paradox was in process, the created, in the form of man, was

---

[58] Strong's Concordance, 4579. Seió, σείω

ultimately rejecting the creator, but the rest of creation was not in agreement, and it was aching because of this great tragedy.

Simultaneously, in the realm of the spirit, the base of Satan's rebellion, the place where Satan still has his kingdom, was shaken! When Christ shouted on the cross, *"It is finished!"* There was not only a physical earthquake but also a spiritual earthquake, something that Satan had never felt before!

Matthew, who was an eyewitness recorded *"and the rocks rent."* He was talking about the huge boulder around Golgotha. Creation was reacting to the great injustice being meted out to the Savior of the world. But there was victory in the air! Not a small one, but the greatest ever to be seen.

The Greek word used for *"rocks"* is *petra*[59], referring to a (large mass of) rock. The other word used for "rocks" in other places in the Bible is the word *lithos*, which means small stones. On the cross, hung "the large mass God" folded in the broken body of a man, the True Rock, the *Petra*, being broken for the sins of the world! It was not easy; it was an impossible task for a man to perform, but yet, a man had to do it. Hence, God's coming in the form of man to save the world. The word *"rent"* is *schizo*[60], meaning to cleave, to split, to rend, to tear, to violently tear asunder, to fracture terribly.

This was a serious earthquake! It left some permanent changes on the earth's surface. *Steven A. Austin, Ph.D.* who wrote the *Greatest Earthquakes of the Bible* made the following observations "An outcrop of laminated Dead Sea sediment can be seen at Wadi Ze'elim above the southwestern shore of the modern Dead Sea near the fortress of Masada. In this sediment, outcrop is a distinctive one-foot thick "mixed layer" of sediment that is tied strongly to the Qumran earthquake's onshore ground ruptures of 31 B.C. Thirteen

---

[59] Strong's Concordance, 4073. Petra, πέτρα
[60] Strong's Concordance, 4977. Schizó, σχίζω

inches above the 31 B.C. event bed is another distinctive "mixed layer" less than one inch thick. The sedimentation rate puts this second earthquake about 65 years after the 31 B.C. earthquake. It seems that the crucifixion earthquake of 33 A.D. was magnitude 5.5, leaving direct physical evidence in a thin layer of disturbed sediment from the Dead Sea."[61]

Not only the rocks were split that day, the stronghold of Satan's earthly kingdom was split and broken once and for all. O how we need to bask in this victory and freedom! It is ours for the taking.

When we go to preach the gospel, we need to tell people that Satan is defeated and the kingdom of the enemy has fallen. When we pray, and spiritual warfare occurs, we need to operate from the standpoint of this victory. When people hear this and when the enemy is reminded of the truth that he is defeated and that his time on earth will expire shortly, people will be released to believe in God and be freed from the devil's stronghold!

While the earth quaked and the rocks rented on the day of the crucifixion, *"the graves were opened."* (Matthews 27:52) Not all graves, but only some selected ones, the graves of the saints. God handpicked who will go free. The graves opened, but the bodies of the saints were left still until Sunday. People may have seen the graves opened and may have planned to repair them, but God had another miracle waiting.

Matthew said that there was *"a violent earthquake"* on Sunday morning (Matthew 28:2). This one was greater than the one on Friday. I believe it represents the moment when Christ was making His way up from hell. So, *"an angel of the Lord came down from heaven and, going to the tomb, rolled back the stone and sat on it."*(Matthews 28:2) That angel was not there to help the Captain of

---

[61] Steven A. Austin, Ph.D., Greatest Earthquakes of the Bible, http://www.icr.org/article/greatest-earthquakes-bible/

the Lord's Host; it was merely there to "roll out a red carpet' for the Lord as He was getting ready to walk out of the grave victoriously.

Robert Lowry (1826-1899) wrote the wonderful hymn "CHRIST AROSE" with the refrain:

Up from the grave he arose;
with a mighty triumph o'er his foes;
he arose a victor from the dark domain,
and he lives forever, with his saints to reign.
He arose! He arose! Hallelujah! Christ arose![62]

It was at this point that the second miracle of the broken tombs was fulfilled: "many bodies of the saints who had fallen asleep were raised; and coming out of the graves after His resurrection, they went into the holy city and appeared to many."(Matthews 27:52-53)

In raising the saints to life, God the Father testifies that Jesus' death brings immortality and life to those who come to Him in faith.[63] Our hope of life comes from the death of Jesus. He died that we may live. What more appropriate sign of this truth could God give to the world than the opening of graves in and around Jerusalem of those who were faithful to God's word while they lived on earth. They served the Lord with the hope that they will live again, and now they were raised to live forever!

Earlier, many of the people in Bethany heard Jesus declaring at Lazarus' tomb: "I am the resurrection and the life; he who believes in Me will live even if he dies, and everyone who lives and believes in Me will never die," (John 11:25- 26). Now they get to see

---

[62] http://www.hymnsite.com/lyrics/umh322.sht
[63]The Voice of the Open Tombs http://www.biblecourses.com/ English/downloads/pdfs/CrossLessons/053.The_Voice_of_the_Open_T ombs.pdf

this truth in full demonstration. He conquered death and hell! Today, we fight from this point of victory.

The opening of these graves testified that Jesus won the victory over the principalities and powers. Jesus exercised His authority, and the power of death and Hades was conquered and subdued! After the great shout *"It is finished!"* Jesus stormed into hell and broke its power, shaking its authority and its grip. He took *"the keys of death and hell"* when He left the tomb!

The spirits of the saints were dwelling freely in Abraham's Bosom but nevertheless restricted to that realm because Christ did not yet pay the price for the salvation of humanity. However, when Jesus snatched the keys from Satan, He shook the very foundations of hell and released the spirits of the saints as Paul said: *"Wherefore he saith, When he ascended up on high, he led captivity captive, and gave gifts unto men,"* (Ephesians 4:8). Principalities and powers had no authority to prevent the spirits of these saints from coming forth into their bodies and rise from the dead days after their tombs split wide open. This was a part of the victory march of our Victorious King!

God's opening of the graves of the saints meant that Jesus' death, in this final analysis, is for those who believe and obey the Lord, for only those of some saints were opened.[64] The word *"saints"* refers to people who had lived and died doing God's will, before Jesus' death. In other words, the message of the open tombs was that His death had brought redemption to those who had died or those who would die in faith.

On the cross Jesus did die for everyone as the writer of Hebrews says: "But we do see Him who was made for a little while lower than the angels, namely, Jesus, because of the suffering of death crowned with glory and honor, so that by the grace of God He might

---

[64] Ibid

taste death for everyone." (Hebrews 2:9) Nevertheless, Jesus said, before His death, that "many" would enter the broad way that leads to destruction (Matthew 7:13, 14). So Jesus is "to all those who obey Him the source of eternal salvation" (Hebrews 5:9). Therefore, not all will be saved, by their choice.

Through the act of opening of the graves of the saints, God declared the eternal nature of the salvation that was brought into the world by Christ. It was the Old Testament saints that came forth from the graves, for they looked forward to the death of Christ. But, when Jesus offered Himself for the sins of the world, the efficacy of His blood sufficed for both the Old Testament saints who died before Him and all New Testament saints who will die after Him. Because of this great work wrought on the cross of Calvary, you and I have a glorious hope of a wonderful resurrection.

The grave cannot withstand the power of God. The earth cannot hold its dead. The sea cannot retain its captives. No power on earth or in hell can hold the bodies of those for whom Christ died for. The power of the grave was broken once and forever on the cross. This is the testimony of the opened graves.[65] It is from this reference point we fight!

So we see a great paradox in the cross; while Jesus, the Son of Man, was being put to death by the cruelty of this world, at the same time He, the Son of God, was made alive in Spirit.

Peter, who was a bit out of touch earlier that day, had deep spiritual insight later on when he wrote "For Christ also suffered once for sins, the righteous for the unrighteous, to bring you to God. He was put to death in the body but made alive in the Spirit." (1 Pet. 3:18). On the surface, many saw the dying Savior, but only a few understood later that He was being made "alive in the Spirit." Once

---

[65] Gordon H. Girod, Words and Wonders of the Cross, Grand Rapids, Mich.: Baker Book House, 1962), 139.

the human part of Christ fulfilled the requirements of the horrible cross, the divine part of Him took control of the situation. In the flesh, He was dying, but in His divinity, He was being made alive, in the Spirit.

Now, since we do not know all that literally happened during the next three days that followed after Christ's death, for a short moment I will suggest a probable visual scenario of what transpired. I'll call it...

"To Hell and Back!"

Joseph and Nicodemus prepared Jesus' body for burial, and in the presence of Mary Magdalene and Mary the mother of Jesus, they did the customary burial in Joseph's *"own new tomb, which he had hewn out in the rock; and he rolled a large stone against the entrance of the tomb and went away."*(Mat. 27:60, Jn. 19:38, 39) However, by that time, in the spirit realm, the Lord was already wreaking havoc in hell, He began proclaiming the gospel to the spirits in prison in Hades (1 Pet. 3:19). For three days and three nights, He moved majestically through the tunnels of this dark abyss with absolutely no assistance from Heaven.

At first, Michael the Archangel, seeing what was happening, may have offered his personal help and that of his legions from heaven. Gabriel too, even though he is no warrior, was probably prepared to take up arms to stand with his King; the two thirds of the angels who resisted Satan's assault on God were probably prepared to join forces as well, for they all must have heard what a terrible place hell is and were concerned for their King. But, He, being the Captain of the Lord's Host took on this battle alone. For there is no *"salvation in any other: for there is none other name under heaven given among men, whereby we must be saved."*(Acts 4:12) If He received help from anyone else, Satan could have cried foul, but the Lord was well able to do this alone. Jesus probably appreciated the offers, but justice required that He faced Satan with all of his cohorts alone.

Yes, one Man facing all of hell, in the heat, in the darkness, in the stench of rotten, burning flesh!

By this time, the news of what happened on the cross had already reached the bottom most part of hell, and full understanding of His Person and purpose had come to the occupants of this dark domain. They were enraged with anger towards Satan for the lies he told them and how he deceived them in the first place, and at the same time they were insanely upset with themselves for disobeying God, but they are also furiously conscious of the fact that it was too late and their fate was already decided; there is no possibility for salvation from this dark, foul-smelling, irritatingly mad, hopeless, never-ending abyss.

Sadness and shame filled the environment, and many demons and sinful men were crying "if only …" "if only …" while beating their heads violently with each requesting that his neighbor destroy him, they quickly found that this was impossible.
But the Lord observed their predicament, all by their own choice to reject the ways of God. His heart was steady and focused. He probably thought within Himself "This is it Father, the final rounds, no more disrespect to you from this old devil and his cohorts."

Satan, in utter shame, wishing that he was never created, crawls up to the front with his large ego crushed, downed his head in almost unbearable disgrace, but still clinging on to "the keys." Unchallenged, Christ reached out to yank the keys out of his hands, but Satan grabs them with both hands as if he was holding on to his very life, but Jesus subdued him and retrieved the keys.

It finally became obvious to Satan, that he now had nothing to bargain with, he had lost the keys! He has no legal rights over humanity anymore; Jesus had paid the price for man's sins. He lost all hopes of ever challenging God again. He feels so much shame that he wishes he can annihilate himself only to remember that this is impossible. He must live as the same lying, shameful, disgusting, defeated creature forever and ever. He knew then that his days are numbered, but made an inner vow to make life as miserable as it can get for every human, as long as he could. He was not going to crawl on his belly, like an old serpent, he will occupy the heavenlies and continue to wage war from above and below as if he still had the authority to do so.

In the moments that followed, Jesus was back on earth. His Spirit now enters His transformed body; He puts on His priestly garment, exits the opened tomb and greets the angels sitting there! "Wow! Said the angel "What a great ending, or rather, what a great beginning for us!"

That was a partly fictitious short story of *"To Hell and Back"* according to Dr. Shiwnandan.

Now, let us move from this picturesque scenario back to sound matured practical theology again.

"Keys of Hell and of Death"

The *"keys of hell and of death."*(Revelations 1:18) are not literal keys, like our car keys, they represent symbols of authority. This understanding is absolutely necessary for successful spiritual warfare; because faulty theology will bear defeat rather than victory against the enemy.

When Adam sinned, Satan did not literally steal a key from him, because Adam never had any keys in the first place. What Adam had was the authority and dominion God gave him. *"And God said, Let us make man in our image, after our likeness: and let them have dominion over the fish of the sea, and over the fowl of the air, and over the cattle, and over all the earth, and over every creeping thing that creepeth upon the earth,"*(Genesis 1:26). Ironically, before God made man He had dominion over everything, but when He made man He did not share dominion with him; instead, He gave it to man.

Therefore, *"dominion over the fish of the sea, and over the fowl of the air, and over the cattle, and over all the earth, and over every creeping thing that creepeth upon the earth."* was not God's anymore, but man's.

When Adam sinned, he became a slave to Satan, and the authority that God gave to him was taken away. From that point onwards, Adam and his generations of humans became slaves and debtors to Satan. Because Adam agreed to disobey God in the garden, the very dominion that man had was transferred to Satan. This authority in the realm of God's governance is what is referred to as *"the keys."*

It was a complete scheme of deceit that Satan used to get *"the keys"* from Adam:

Firstly, using the power of suggestion, Satan deceived the serpent into thinking that since it was *"more subtle than any beast of the field which the Lord God had made"* (Genesis 3:1), it could perhaps become greater than the man who God made in His image, the same day it was created also. The only way it could achieve dominance over man is to successfully convince him to disobey God, by eating from the fruit of the forbidden tree. What the serpent did not realize, is that in its association with the old devil, Satan, it was exposed to the risk that Satan would use its innate characteristics and potential to bring its own downfall and to foil the plan of God for humanity and the world at large.

Being *"more subtle than any beast of the field"* did not necessarily mean that the serpent had enough superb intelligence to negotiate with Satan, it was falling into a trap. It allowed itself to be used to deceive the woman. What it should have done was not to have any association with this intruder in the first place, and it was, for this reason, it was judged severely by God. From God's standpoint, it was wise enough not to be negotiating with the enemy of God and not to question God's sovereign laws for man. God did not allow the fact of Satan's deception to overrule the responsibility of the serpent to resist the devil. God said to the serpent: *"Because thou hast done this, thou art cursed above all cattle, and above every beast of the field; upon thy belly shalt thou go, and dust shalt thou eat all the days of thy life."*(Genesis 3:14)

Secondly, Satan deceived the woman. Using the power of supernatural speech, Satan captured the woman's attention. It might have been a Wow moment for Eve; she may have never heard an animal speak before. Then came the deception, *"Yea, hath God said, Ye shall not eat of every tree of the garden?"*(Genesis 3:1) Eve replied: *"We may eat of the fruit of the trees of the garden: But of the fruit of the tree which is in the midst of the garden, God hath said, Ye shall not eat of it, neither shall ye touch it, lest ye die."*

Then, Satan tricked the woman and the man into thinking that they would be perhaps equal to or greater than God. He said: "For God doth know that in the day ye eat thereof, then your eyes shall be opened, and ye shall be as gods, knowing good and evil. And when the woman saw that the tree was good for food and that it was pleasant to the eyes, and a tree to be desired to make one wise, she took of the fruit thereof, and did eat, and gave also unto her husband with her; and he did eat,"(Genesis 3:5,6). Satan knew exactly what would have happened, because he fell from grace for the same reason, exalting himself on the same level like God. And, Satan knew that if Adam failed to serve God through obedience, Adam will become his slave through disobedience. By his choice, as Satan suspected would happen, Adam ate of the tree of knowledge of good and evil and fell.

Satan felt ecstatic and leaped for joy because this gave him a chance to rise above man and to have dominion over him and his generations to come. What a win this was for Satan, he finally got *"the keys"* of authority over man, God's crown creation.

There was nothing Adam could have done during his lifetime, to get back that authority from Satan. Nor, was there anything his forthcoming generations could have done to wrestle *"the keys"* from this formidable enemy. So the spiritual enslavement of humanity continued from generation to generation, it would have continued forever if Christ did not go to the cross.

Jesus' death on Calvary's cross was the only method, as hideous as it was, for humanity to be bought back to God. The price for *"the keys"* was the life of God's Son. And, who was He buying humanity back from? Their legal owner, Satan! But thank God Jesus did, for Romans 5:19 says, *"For as by one man's disobedience many were made sinners, so by the obedience of one shall many be made righteous."* Hallelujah!

The imputed righteousness of Christ in our lives enables us to stand and walk in the victory of the cross. We have been justified on the basis of the righteousness of Christ to stand free in God's presence and be victorious over Satan. Justification brings about a change in our standing before God, not a change in our own rightness before God. We do not become inherently righteous in justification; instead, we gain positional righteousness on the basis of the victory Christ wroth on the cross. This is a fact that we must never forget because it is the very foundation for our standing in spiritual warfare. He took *"the keys,"* now we have the rights to use them.

Justification is not ontological; it does not change who we are in terms of our sinful nature. We are still fallen and will remain so until we are glorified. Therefore, we must always be on guard for temptations and evil intrusions, along our path to maintain our victory in Christ. Because we are able to stand on the victory of Christ, we can fight from victory! We are not trying to win a war; we are enacting the victory of a battle that was already won 2000 years ago. Our Victor shouted, *"It is finished!"* Now, we must be able to shout with Him *"It is finished for me!"*

14. We are more than Conquerors, We are Overcomers

God promises His people that He will work in and through them so that they can experience victory over Satan:

"These things I have spoken to you, so that in Me you may have peace. In the world you have tribulation, but take courage; I have overcome the world."(Jn. 16:33) Jesus is saying that He has overcome "the world," which does not mean the physical realm that contains the planetary bodies, but rather, the "world system" or the fleshly and satanic standards that influence one, contrary to the Word and ways of God. "In the world, you have tribulation" which means that every believer will be tested and tried, so they must ultimately conquer, subdue, and be victorious over the ways of the world. We will be either "overcomers" or "overtaken." An "overcomer" is someone who successfully conquers, subdues and has victory over the world; the "overtaken" are themselves conquered and subdued by the world.

"Ye are of God, little children, and have overcome them: because greater is he that is in you, than he that is in the world." (1 Jn.4:4) We are overcomers because we have Christ in us. This means that we live faithfully according to His Word and ways.

"For whatever is born of God overcomes the world; and this is the victory that has overcome the world -- our faith. And who is the one who overcomes the world, but he who believes that Jesus is the Son of God?" (1 Jn. 5:4-5)

Overcoming is always a venture of *"faith."* It is faithfulness to put God's Word and ways into practice, which defines someone who is *"born of God"* and who have the possibility to overcome the world. Without faith, there will be a lack of substance in one's spirit, which translates to lack of victory over the world.

"Do not be overcome by evil, but overcome evil with good." (Rom. 12:21) Our personal conditions affect our personal actions! If personally we are *"overcome by evil,"* we will find it difficult to *"overcome evil with good."* We must be experiencing an overcoming nature in order to perform overcoming actions. The corollary is also true. If we take the time to constantly *"overcome evil with good,"* we will *"not be overcome by evil."* This is spiritual warfare on a personal level. This helps us to appropriate the overcoming victory of the cross in our lives.

Overcoming is the process of gaining practical victory in the spiritual battle that encompasses a conflict against Satan and all the corresponding elements of the world-system's values and behavior which he infiltrates. But, it is not only warring against evil; it is the biblical response to evil by choosing to do biblical good. It is not only identifying and countering the direct antics and tactics of Satan, but also his indirect working through false prophets, false teachers and their associated works of deception, even within the church. Our only chance for sustained victory is to become identified and enslaved to Christ by putting His Word and ways into practice, and abiding in Him alone through faith.

Our Victorious Lord has given many scenarios of overcomers and their ultimate victory in the real stories of the churches of Asia, in the Book of Revelations.

Overcomers in the 7 Churches in Asia

In His messages to the seven Churches of Asia, in the Book of Revelation, the Lord taught that successful spiritual warriors would be rewarded by Him.

To the Church at Ephesus He said: *"To him who overcomes, I will give the right to eat from the tree of life which is in the paradise of God."(Rev.2:7)* Wow! Is this the same *"tree of life"* which Adam passed off eating from? Yes, it might be the very one even though there is more than one *"tree of life"* in Heaven. (Rev. 22:2)

So what happened to the *"tree of life"* that was in Eden? God guarded it for a while in the Garden of Eden after Adam sinned, but then, He transferred it to Heaven for overcomers to enjoy. For Adam, eating of the tree of life (Genesis 2:9; 3:22- 23) would have meant committing himself to going God's way in faith and obedience, then ultimately be given the gift of living forever. So if Adam and Eve had eaten from *"the tree of life"* after they sinned, they would have to live forever in that sinful state in the sin-cursed world, with no hope of heaven. But God had a better plan in place; one of redemption in Jesus Christ with a new heaven and new earth that would not be touched by the curse. Praise God!

For overcoming Christians, however, we would have already gained eternal life through our faith in Christ Jesus when we will be given a chance to *"eat from the tree of life which is in the paradise of God."* Therefore, eating from that tree will not have the same benefit for us, but it will nevertheless be a beautiful experience to eat what God created for the first man!

From the church at Ephesus, we learn that overcomers who are faithful and consistent to the end will experience the eternal rewards of their salvation in Christ.

To the Church at Smyrna, the Lord counseled "Be faithful, even to the point of death, and I will give you the crown of life." (Rev. 2:10) Then He said, "He who overcomes will not be hurt at all by the second death." (Rev. 2:11) In this statement, He was really referring to "the fiery lake of burning sulfur."(Rev. 21:8) Implied in the Lord's message to this church is no promise of deliverance from natural death or martyrdom. Is He saying that Warriors must be willing to fight to the death? I think He is!

The believers must remain steadfast and true to the cause of Christ, throughout their walk on earth. For the Scriptures says "Blessed and holy are those who have taken part in the first resurrection. The second death has no power over them, but they will be priests of God and of Christ and will reign with him for a thousand years," (Rev.20:6). Wearing the crown of life and reigning with Christ are special rewards for successfully overcoming warfare.

From the Church at Smyrna, we learn that overcomers can endure even the worst earthly circumstances because their gaze is fixed on eternity.

To the Church at Pergamum the Lord says: "To him who overcomes, I will give some of the hidden manna. I will also give him a white stone with a new name written on it, known only to him who receives it." (Rev. 2:17) Why all of these rewards? Well, Pergamum wasn't an easy place to live and minister in; Christian soldiers had to be on alert constantly. Pergamum was one of the most important cities in the Roman Empire. It was about 70 miles north of Smyrna. It was known throughout the world for its architectural innovations, including the temple of Athena, the great altar to Zeus, and a library that held over 200, 000 volumes of books. By the time the Lord spoke to this church, Pergamum had become not only a key political center but a major intellectual and religious center as well, with a plethora of cultic philosophies and spiritualties existing there. The Lord's description of the situation for the Christians was "I know where you live—where Satan has his throne."(Rev. 2:13)

From his throne there, Satan may have tried to carry out his diabolical plan by using the ungodly political powers to persecute God's people, through forcing them to accept the pagan religions, to make sacrifices and offerings to the gods, and to declare that Caesar is Lord and Savior. However, the brethren refused to be sucked into the system and *"they overcame him by the blood of the Lamb, and by the word of their testimony, and they loved not their lives unto the death,"* (Rev. 12:11), Jesus commends the church for remaining true to His name and refusing to renounce its faith in Him. Hence, *"the hidden manna... a white stone with a new name written on it" (Rev. 2:17)* Jesus is the true manna from heaven (Jn. 6:48-51). Receiving the hidden manna speaks of an increased capacity to feed on Jesus as the Word through all eternity. It promises an increased capacity to enjoy the Word in the age to come. While the white stone is a reward of remembrance for unusual dedication to Jesus, it may tell the story of our love for Jesus and how it moved Him. I imagine that the white stone will probably be a precious stone, which will be one of our most valued possessions in the age to come. The Lord will reward the faithful overcoming Christians among us similarly. Hallelujah!

From the Church at Pergamum, we learn that overcomers are sustained by God's Word, and their exclusive devotion to Christ alone.

To the Church at Thyatira, the Lord said: "To him who overcomes and does my will to the end, I will give authority over the nations— 'He will rule them with an iron scepter; he will dash them to pieces like pottery.' Just as I have received authority from my Father. I will also give him the morning star," (Rev. 2:26-28).

Thyatira was founded by one of the successors of Alexander the Great, named Seleucus. As with Smyrna and Pergamum, the Bible does not record the founder of the church at Thyatira. However, it is believed that this church was probably founded as an outreach of Paul's ministry at Ephesus (Acts 19:10). The church was commended by the Lord for five virtues: love, service, faithfulness, perseverance and good works, (Rev. 2:19) but, it was guilty of one sin. They tolerated the destructive influence of the spirit of Jezebel by allowing the false teachings by an influential prophetess. Most in the church, maybe the pastor also, were aware of a destructive force within their midst, but they lacked the spiritual courage to confront this strong personality with the false doctrines.

Nevertheless, there was a remnant there, whom the Lord Jesus identified as *"the rest of you,"* who did not hold on to Jezebel's teaching but resisted it. The Lord singled out these faithful overcomers and said to them, *"But that which ye have already hold fast till I come."* (Rev. 2:25) Through the faithful resistance of this remnant, Jesus highlighted two eternal rewards to motivate us: leadership over the nations with Him, and the morning star (Rev. 2:26-28).

Power over the nations refers to, having leadership positions over the nations during the millennial reign with Jesus in the earth, (Luke. 19:11-27; Rev. 3:21). However, this promise of ruling also refers to ushering Kingdom rulership on the earth now! And, it may be speaking to leadership through eternity.

The morning star speaks of Jesus as *"the bright Morning Star,"* (Rev. 22:16). Giving us the morning star means promising to increase our capacity, to have greater spiritual encounters with Him through His Spirit. The knowledge of this reward assures us that what we do for love now is remembered by Jesus. Whatever it takes, we must fight against false teachings that Satan tries to inject into the Body of Christ.

From the Church at Thyatira, we learn that overcomers who effectively war against immorality, idolatry, and heresies come out as victors.

To the Church at Sardis, the Lord said: "He who overcomes will like them be dressed in white. I will never blot out his name from the book of life but will acknowledge his name before my Father and his angels," (Rev. 3:5). What is it they had to overcome? Well, the church at Sardis didn't suffer from the same kinds of problems that affected the churches at Ephesus, Smyrna, Pergamos, and Thyatira. These were situated in communities that were actively hostile to the truth and were challenged to one degree or another with false doctrine. They all had both internal and external problems. However, for Sardis, both the city and the church enjoyed relative peace.

The city of Sardis was a kind of elite city of Asia Minor, which stood fifteen hundred feet above sea level, on the top of a mountain in the Tmolus range that had almost perpendicular sides. It was well guarded and enjoyed relative peace compared to its counterparts. This church also enjoyed the relative calm of the general area and took on some of the characteristics of the city.

Unlike the preceding churches which were commended by the Lord for their works, the Church at Sardis was told: *"I know thy works, that thou hast a name that thou livest, and art dead,"* (Rev. 3:1). Unlike the other churches which were struggling and fighting just to continue being alive and focused, the church at Sardis had become stagnant, apathetic and lethargic in its service of the Lord, and as a result no longer deserved the reputation of being alive. Peace, which should have been a tremendous blessing for the church became a source of lethargy and deadness. The church at Sardis had no problems because it was not doing anything in the community that anyone objected to. This was an unusual situation, which may indirectly mean that the church was not challenging the system of the day. No objection meant no fight, so no spiritual warfare was taking place. This was unpleasing to God.

But, the One who "hath the seven Spirits of God, and the seven stars" (v.1) said to the church "Be watchful, and strengthen the things which remain, that are ready to die:" (v. 2) "Remember therefore how thou hast received and heard, and hold fast, and repent."(v.3) Their problem was in actuality inward, so their warfare has to focus on dealing with the enemy of lethargy and compromise. Prayerlessness and laziness might have also been involved, so the Lord was asking them to rise up and fight on several levels, in which their lives were secretly assaulted by the enemy. He also told them to use the Word to find victory and life. The word of God not only minister's life to those who are spiritually dead, but it also strengthens life in those whom Christ has already made alive.

To those who were ready to heed the Lord's rebuke and counsel, He said: *"He who overcomes will like them be dressed in white. I will never blot out his name from the book of life, but will acknowledge his name before my Father and his angels."* (Rev. 3:5) White refers not only to purity, festal joy, and victory but to the lustrous glory we shall be covered with. "I will never blot out his name from the book of life," He promised these victors that they will truly and securely possess life forever. However, this passage also implies that some names shall be blotted out from the book of life. Some who, as a result of their adoption and regeneration through the blood of Jesus, were entitled to and fitted for eternal life. While others, through falling from grace, lose these blessings and come under guilt, condemnation, and wrath again. A frightening thought, but a true one nevertheless. Some in the churches of Sardis may have experienced this. It is the overcomers that win!

To the Church at Philadelphia, the Lord said: *"Him who overcomes I will make a pillar in the temple of my God. Never again will he leave it. I will write on him the name of my God and the name of the city of my God, the new Jerusalem, which is coming down out of heaven from my God, and I will also write on him my new name."* (Rev. 3:12)

As in the case of Smyrna, there is nothing bad said about the Church at Philadelphia. They have the *"key of David"* which the Lord will use, so He *"that openeth, and no man shutteth; and shutteth, and no man openeth."*

The Lord says to this church that He knows they have little strength of their own, but He also knows that they have not denied His Name. To deny His Name would have disqualified them for the prize of the high calling of God (Phil. 3:14). In other words, they had faithfully and obediently rested on God's Spirit even through the difficult times, (2 Cor. 13:4). And, because of their faithfulness to keep the *"word of My patience,"* He will keep them from the very hour of temptation that is to come upon the earth. He will also make those who say they are Jews, but are not, bow at their feet. God exhorts them to *"hold fast to that which you have, so no one will take your crown."*

The Lord's promise to the faithful and obedient overcomer, in the church of Philadelphia, is that He will make them a pillar in His temple. A pillar is symbolic of a steadfast figure of strength and durability. Thus, these faithful saints will remain secure and firm in their positions of strength at the Lord's side and enjoy tremendous intimacy with Him. Because of this intimacy, they will not go out of the sanctuary anymore. The Lord says He will also write upon them the Name of God, the name of the city of God (Jerusalem) and also His own name.

The lesson we learn from the church of Philadelphia is that overcomers discern that everything accomplished for the Kingdom of Christ is rooted in eternity, even the seasons of accomplishment in this life. Therefore, they must take their eyes off the temporal things and focus on the eternal - let Christ be our focus.

To the Church at Laodicea the Lord said: "To him who overcomes, I will give the right to sit with me on my throne, just as I overcame and sat down with my Father on his throne," (Rev. 3:21).

Laodicea represents the last-days church, which is neither *"hot nor cold."* The focus is on people rather than the Lord. This is "seeker friendly "rather than "Jesus friendly" so the Lord said: *"Behold, I stand at the door and knock. If anyone hears My voice and opens the door, I will come in to him and dine with him, and he with Me"* (Rev.3:20). The music and worship programs create excitement, but the Lord is not present. The message is charged with human wisdom, but it is so watered down that it does not stimulate a renewed personal commitment of obedience and faithfulness to the Lord. The church says it is rich and in need of nothing, but in truth and from God's perspective, they are *"wretched, miserable, poor, blind and naked."* But there are some faithful believers. God's promise to the faithful and obedient overcomer in the Laodicea church is that Christ will let them sit with Him on His Throne. In other words, the overcomers in this church will have a "joint participation" in the throne room of the King, (Rev. 3:21).

So, the lesson we learn from the church at Laodicea is that overcomers are ensured that it is Christ who will always and exclusively be seated upon the throne of their lives. Wow! What an assurance, the struggle will be over!

Now, as we take the seven churches into consideration, it seems like the rewards for overcoming move upwards, from the wonderful blessings for the overcomers in the Church of Ephesus to incredible blessings for the overcomers in the Church of Laodicea. These extraordinary promises should be incentives for all of us to strive, press on, struggle, contend, engage in warfare and labor to become faithful overcomers in Christ.

Overcoming: Past, Present, and Future

The seven churches in Revelation 2 and 3 were literal churches in Asia Minor (Turkey) at the writing of Revelation in A.D. 96. Though they were literal churches in that time, there is also spiritual significance for those churches and believers today. The first purpose of the letters was to communicate with the literal churches and meet their needs at that time. The second purpose is to reveal seven different types of individuals/churches throughout history and instruct them on God's truth.

A possible third purpose is to use the seven churches to foreshadow seven different periods in the history of the Church.[66] However, each of the seven churches describes issues that could fit the Church in any time in its history. So, although there may be some truth to the seven churches representing seven eras, this point should not be stretched too far. Our focus should be on what message God is giving us through the seven churches, in relation to living for Him and overcoming.

Today, we can be overcomers similar to the brethren mentioned in Revelations. The Greek word commonly translated *"overcome"* is *nikaó*:[67] to conquer, prevail, to win a victory, to stand victorious over an enemy.

Inwardly, to "overcome," means to live in the victory of Jesus Christ. It means to live in victory over sin and Satan and to live in victory under the new nature in Christ, by appropriating through practical living, the victory purchased by Jesus on the cross.   Overcoming involves warfare. I must stand in the victory of Jesus Christ, refusing the old, and yielding to the new. I must do this, for God will not do this for me. When God talks about *"He that overcometh,"* He is talking about someone who believes that the victory over the enemy is already finished by Jesus Christ. He is talking about someone who, because of this faith, has obeyed God, and has taken possession of areas of his life that were formerly occupied and controlled by the old nature. *"He that overcomes"* is a qualifying mark given to those who are to reign and rule with Jesus Christ.

---

66 What do the seven churches in Revelation stand for?,
https://www.gotquestions.org/seven-churches-Revelation.html
67 Strong's 3528. nikaónikaó: to conquer, prevail, νικάω

Externally, overcoming means standing on the victory Jesus Christ won on the cross. I can overcome Satan because Christ has already secured that victory. Overcoming, therefore, is, standing on the platform of the cross and shouting *"It is finished."* Our warfare is never to win ground; to win the victory. Our warfare is to hold ground, to enact the victory because we already possess the victory in Jesus Christ. When God talks about *"he that overcometh,"* He is talking about someone who believes that the victory over the enemy is already finished by Jesus Christ. He is talking about someone who, because of this faith, has obeyed God, and has taken possession of areas beyond his life that were formerly occupied and controlled by the old Devil; Satan. True overcomers take back their families, their church, their communities and nations for Christ. True overcomers take back what the devil stole.

Overcoming is a Possibility!

Overcoming the Strongman will never be a simple task. He has been fighting this battle against God for several millennia now. He is very skillful in counteracting the plans and purposes of God, right from the very beginning. When God created the angels, Lucifer deceived one-third of them to rebel against God (Isa. 14:12–15, Rev. 12:4). So God countered that move by creating man in His own image, *"a little lower than the angels"* (Ps. 8:5) but Satan tempted Adam and Eve to sin and took *"the keys"* of authority from man. Through His mercy and love, God countered that action by providing a redemptive covering for Adam and Eve so they could return to fellowship with Him, but Satan tried to counteract that move again by getting Cain to kill Abel in order to cut off the godly line.

This war of moves and counter moves has continued throughout the Old Testament between the Creator and the defeated. Yet, the stubborn and determined creature is bent on having his own way.

So God finally, *"in the fullness of time"* (Gal. 5:5) presented His King who Satan thought was a pawn. In the principle of war, the deceiver was deceived! When Jesus came on the scene, Satan tried his usual tactics by tempting Jesus in the wilderness, (Matt. 4:1–11) but the Lord overcame him by using the Word of God. Satan then made what he thought was the final move at the cross; killing Jesus and thinking he had gotten rid of Him. However, it was the Father who had the final move by raising Jesus from the dead with *"the keys"* in His hand!

Now, Jesus gave the *"keys"* to the church. Today, the *"keys"* move is our move! No matter what's going on in your world, Jesus' bodily resurrection was God's top move; it was God's trump card! As spiritual warriors and overcomers, this is our footing for victory over the Strongman. We need to continually assert ourselves in the Living Christ, take up the full armor of God and stand in victory.

Let us keep the six realities of spiritual warfare discussed in this book constantly before us:
1. The Spirit World can be seen.
2. Truth Wins
3. Vision affects Outcome
4. Satan Wants To Win
5. Don't Be Afraid of the Enemy
6. We Fight from Victory to Victory!

God has set up a system of victory for every believer in the realm of the spirit. Spiritual overcomers must know how to navigate the spiritual realm like a pilot knows how to navigate the sky. The pilot uses his knowledge and instruments; we use the Word of God and spiritual perception.

The ills of this world are generally seen in the physical realm, but they originate from the spiritual realm. Overcomers engage in battle in the invisible spiritual world, which is responsible for the battles in the visible, physical world. But, it is very possible to overcome and win, because our blessings are located in the heavenly realms.

"Blessed be the God and Father of our Lord Jesus Christ, who hath blessed us with all spiritual blessings in heavenly places in Christ:" (Eph. 1:3). Everything God is going to do for us is located in the unseen realm, so we have to be comfortable operating at this level to be successful.

Then, in Ephesians 1:20, Paul says that the Risen Christ, our Overcoming Captain is seated in that very realm. To flow with Him, we must flow in that realm. Actually, we as believers have also been raised with Christ, and are also seated *"in the heavenly realms"* (Eph. 2:6). So God put the whole package together. Our real problems originate from the spiritual realm, and the solutions we need emanate from the spiritual realm where our blessings are, where Jesus is, and where we are also located, in our spirits.

Nevertheless, we cannot assert our position in Christ, and at the same time be careless in letting down our gloves, because the devil has assigned at least one demon to every believer's life, to work on our weak spots. Even though they cannot know our thoughts, they can review the patterns of our actions and have an idea of our thinking. They would then exploit those areas, sins, and weaknesses to bring us down and cause us to live in defeat instead of victory. However, we are not alone; God has also assigned at least one angel to each one of us, to operate on our behalf in the spirit realm. *"For he shall give his angels charge over thee, to keep thee in all thy ways,"* (Ps. 91:11). So, in our daily walk, there are those that are for us and those that are against us. Therefore, let us live in the spirit so as not to fulfill the lust of the flesh.

We can walk and live in overcoming victory because the only power that Satan and his demons have over you and me is the power we give them. Remember that Jesus gave us *"the keys"* Satan is already a defeated foe; he was crushed at the cross and the empty tomb of Christ! To operate, Satan and his cohorts need our permission to unleash his forces in our lives. They operate by consent and by cooperation. No consent and no cooperation means no operation, because we have *"the keys"* that *"Whatsoever ye shall bind on earth shall be bound in heaven: and whatsoever ye shall loose on earth shall be loosed in heaven."*(Mt. 18:18)

Overcome the Strongman!

References:

1. Arnold, Clinton E. (1997). 3 crucial questions about spiritual warfare. Grand Rapids, Mich.: Baker Publishing Group. p. 17. ISBN 0801057841.
2. 2.Statement on Spiritual Warfare, https://www.lausanne.org/content/statement/statement-on-spiritual-warfare-1993
3. Carl Moeller, "North Korea Spiritual Warfare: Insights from Carl Moeller," Christian Broadcasting Network, 12-3-2010
4. Spiritual warfare, https://en.wikipedia.org/wiki/Spiritual_warfare
5. Ibid
6. McAlister, Elizabeth (2012-04-25). "From Slave Revolt to a Blood Pact with Satan: The Evangelical Rewriting of Haitian History". Studies in Religion/Sciences
7. Spiritual warfare, https://en.wikipedia.org/wiki/Spiritual_warfare
8. https://www.lausanne.org/content/covenant/lausanne-covenant
9. Strong's Concordance, 1743. Endunamoó - "be strong."
10. http://www.primaryhomeworkhelp.co.uk/romans/officers.html
11. http://christianmomthoughts.com/what-is-the-difference-between-absolute-and-relative-truth/
12. Ibid
13. Ibid
14. Webster's New World College Dictionary
15. http://www.erictyoung.com/2010/09/15/developing-practical-righteousness-%E2%80%94-john-macarthur/
16. https://heavenawaits.wordpress.com/different-levels-of-faith-%E2%80%93-where-are-you/
17. https://en.wikipedia.org/wiki/Category:Roman_swords
18. http://www.swordhistory.info/?p=120
19. http://www.christianarsenal.com/Christian_Arsenal/Full_Armor_of_God.html
20. Ibid
21. Armed and Able to Stand ??
22. Ibid
23. http://biblehub.com/commentaries/maclaren/ephesians/
24. Ibid

25. The Expositor's Dictionary of Texts
26. Elizabeth Howell, How Many Galaxies Are There? https://www.space.com/25303-how-many-galaxies-are-in-the-universe.html
27. The New Age Movement, http://www.watchman.org/profiles/pdf/newageprofile.pdf
28. New Age or Old Occult?*- Biblical Discernment Ministries - Revised 11/01
29. Ibid
30. http://christianity.about.com/od/glossary/a/Postmodernism.htm)
31. http://www.dictionary.com/browse/theism.
32. (http://www.gty.org/resources/Articles/A379/What-Is-Truth)
33. http://www.merriam-webster.com
34. (http://www.psychologydiscussion.net/perception/perception-meaning-definition-principles-and-factors-affecting-in-perception/634)
35. Constitution of WHO: principles http://who.int/about/mission/en/
36. Cognitive Psychology & Its Applications , http://cranepsych.edublogs.org/files/2009/06/Factors_perception.pdf
37. How To Teach Effectively, http://lyceumbooks.com/pdf/howtoteacheffectively_typesoflearners.pdf
38. https://www.merriam-webster.com/dictionary/imagination
39. http://military.wikia.com/wiki/Fort_Zeelandia_ (Guyana)
40. 40.http://www.truthnet.org/Spiritual-warfare/8Spiritual-Strongholds/Strongholds-spiritual.htm
41. Ibid
42. http://www.israel-a-history-of.com/walls-of-jericho.html
43. Ibid
44. https://www.thoughtco.com/constantinople-capital-of-eastern-roman-empire-119706
45. http://pastorrick.com/devotional/english/principles-for-personal-change-strongholds
46. https://www.unicef.org/immunization/index_why.html
47. https://www.statista.com/statistics/265002/deaths-due-to-lack-of-vaccination-in-2002/
48. https://www.guttmacher.org/fact-sheet/induced-abortion-worldwide
49. Bodie Hodge, Harvard, Yale, Princeton, Oxford — Once

Christian? June 27, 2007,
https://answersingenesis.org/christianity/harvard-yale-princeton-oxford-once-christian/

50. Jeff Sagnip Oct 6, 2016, New Report Shows 62 Million "Missing" Girls in China Thanks to Sex-Selection Abortions, http://www.lifenews.com/2016/10/06/new-report-shows-62-million-missing-girls-in-china-thanks-to-sex-selection-abortions/

51. What is Christian Persecution? https://www.opendoorsusa.org/christian-persecution/

52. Guyana/Venezuela 1899 Arbitral Award http://guyanachronicle.com/2016/10/09/guyanavenezuela-1899-arbitral-award

53. Israeli–Palestinian conflict https://en.wikipedia.org/wiki/Israeli%E2%80%93Palestinian_conflict

54. Healing of the Spirit Booklet, http://healingofthespirit.org/our-ministry/healing-of-the-spirit-booklet/ Territorial Spirits PDF

55. Strong's Concordance, 4655. Skotos, σκότος

56. Strong's Concordance, 1093. Gé, γῆ, γῆς, ἡ

57. Strong's Concordance, 4579. Seió, σείω

58. Strong's Concordance, 4073. Petra, πέτρα

59. Strong's Concordance, 4977. Schizó, σχίζω

60. Steven A. Austin, Ph.D., Greatest Earthquakes of the Bible, http://www.icr.org/article/greatest-earthquakes-bible/

61. http://www.hymnsite.com/lyrics/umh322.sht

62. The Voice of the Open Tombs http://www.biblecourses.com/English/downloads/pdfs/CrossLessons/053.The_Voice_of_the_Open_Tombs.pdf

63. Ibid

64. Gordon H. Girod, Words and Wonders of the Cross, Grand Rapids, Mich.: Baker Book House, 1962, 139.

65. What do the seven churches in Revelation stand for? https://www.gotquestions.org/seven-churches-Revelation.html

66. Strong's 3528. nikaónikaó: to conquer, prevail, νικάω

THE AUTHOR

Dr. Ravindra Shiwnandan has been the Senior Pastor of Herstelling Assembly of God Global Outreach Center, and a Practicing Physician at Dr. Shiwnandan's Clinic for more than twenty-two years.

Dr. Shiwnandan is a credentialed holding Pastor with the AOG for more than thirty-two years now. He holds M.B.B.S., Th.M., and D.Min. Degrees serves on the General Presbytery of the AOG and as the Director of the AOG Evangelism Association. He and his wife Dr. Michelle are physicians who believe in whole person salvation and have a robust humanitarian approach to ministry. Together they are the Co-Founders of Herstelling Vocational Skills Training Institute, where hundreds of youths and single parents benefit from free certified skills training. They are also the Co-Founders of Hinterland Medical Missions, taking medical missions teams to various remote locations. Drs. Shiwnandan both serve on the leadership team of Early Pregnancy Advisory Services; an organization that promotes the sanctity of human life and provides free counseling service to women with crises pregnancies.

Dr. Ravindra Shiwnandan received the Prime Minister's Medal for his outstanding performance on completion of his medical degree at the University Of Guyana, School Of Medicine. He continued his career development at Queens University, Canada, Gulf Course Ultrasound Institute, National Procedures Institute and Institute For International Medicine, University of Missouri, Kansas City, USA. With the recent interest in the Oil & Gas Industry, Dr. Shiwnandan qualified to offer services through the Maritime Coastguard Agency, Maritime Labor Convention 2006 and Oil & Gas UK.

For more than twenty years, Dr. Shiwnandan has held professional memberships with the American College of Gastroenterology, the West Indian Association of Gastroenterologists, the Christian Medical Foundation, and the American Association of Pastoral Counselors. Additionally, he has been serving as the Representative of the Medical Community on the Central Board of Health and the Pharmacy and Poisons Board in the Guyana Ministry of Public Health.

As the Country Representative for ISOM, Covent Theological Seminary, and Nation-To-Nation Christian University, Dr. Shiwnandan has seen the creation of more than twenty-nine Church-Based Schools of Ministry, that offer Diplomas and Degrees, organized to train Christian workers for the Kingdom of God.

God is using Dr. Shiwnandan as a powerful, prolific speaker and writer, both on medical and spiritual matters with an aim to fulfill the Great Commission. For more information, kindly call 592 625 9749, or visit www.herstellingaoggoc.org.

Made in the USA
Columbia, SC
25 July 2022